W9-CCR-617

THE MORAL CONTEXT
OF PASTORAL CARE

BOOKS BY DON S. BROWNING
PUBLISHED BY THE WESTMINSTER PRESS

The Moral Context of Pastoral Care
Generative Man: Psychoanalytic Perspectives
Atonement and Psychotherapy

THE
Moral Context
OF
Pastoral Care

DON S. BROWNING

THE WESTMINSTER PRESS
PHILADELPHIA

Copyright © 1976 The Westminster Press

All rights reserved—no part of this book may be
reproduced in any form without permission in writing
from the publisher, except by a reviewer who wishes
to quote brief passages in connection with a review
in magazine or newspaper.

BOOK DESIGN BY DOROTHY E. JONES

PUBLISHED BY THE WESTMINSTER PRESS ®
PHILADELPHIA, PENNSYLVANIA

PRINTED IN THE UNITED STATES OF AMERICA

Library of Congress Cataloging in Publication Data

Browning, Don S
    The moral context of pastoral care.

    Includes bibliographical references.
    1. Pastoral theology—Addresses, essays,
lectures. 2. Pastoral counseling—Addresses,
essays, lectures. I. Title.
BV4011.5.B76   253   76–5858
ISBN 0–664–20742–1

Contents

LINCOLN CHRISTIAN COLLEGE AND SEMINARY

83466

Preface

There is considerable confusion today about the foundations of pastoral care. Where do we get the authority and how do we define the goals of our care for one another in the context of the church? Both ministers and pastoral counseling specialists are less clear about this today than should be the case. This is true for a variety of reasons, not the least of which is the impact of modern psychology and psychotherapy on the life of the contemporary church. I have been one who felt that the pastoral ministry of the church could benefit from a wise use of psychology and psychotherapeutic insights. I still believe this. However, I now believe even more firmly than I once did that to incorporate insights from these disciplines with integrity requires clear understanding of the theological grounds of the church's ministry of care.

Although this book is addressed primarily to the church community, I invite secular counselors and psychotherapists to read it as well. They may learn something about the distant and now almost completely obscured religious foundations of their own work. Although modern psychotherapeutic practices ostensibly have been secularized, there still may be a horizon of religious meaning that surrounds them and that needs to be recognized.

In the following pages I have arranged a series of lectures given over the last three years. The thesis of these lectures is simple: the pastoral care of the Christian churches needs to be understood within the context of the tradition of practical moral rationality typical of ancient Judaism, especially as this developed in later Pharisaic and rabbinical movements. It is important to recognize this context for Christianity in order to clarify the kind of care Christians should offer to one another and to members of the larger society. Without recognizing this contextual background, both Christianity and the care that it extends can become norm-less antinomianism.

Chapters I through V were first given before the faculty and Doctor of Ministry students of Meadville-Lombard Theological School during the spring and autumn of 1972. Most of these same lectures were given as the Scott Lectures at the Graduate Semi-nary of Phillips University during the autumn of 1974. Sections of Chapter VI were given before the plenary session of the Associ-ation for Clinical Pastoral Education at its annual meeting in Atlanta, Georgia, in November 1974.

At the end of an earlier book entitled *Generative Man,* I in-dicated that I someday wanted to compare the image of man that I found in the writings of Erik Erikson with the Christian image of man. The present book is not intended to fulfill that ambition. In the process of writing on the moral psychology of Erik Erikson, however, I did become more sensitized to the moral and ethical dimensions of what I will call the "Judeo-Christian conglomerate." But a more direct confrontation be-tween "generative" and "Christian" man must wait until a later time.

I want to thank Donna Guido, Susan Hopkins, and Jean Baker for typing the manuscript at various stages. I also want to thank Randall Mason and Jim Gibbons for reading certain sections of the manuscript and sharing with me their evaluations. My appre-ciation goes to Lewis Rambo who has, for the second time, helped me with some of the editing for one of my books.

Wives and families must never be excluded. My wife Carol and my children, Beth and Chris, have taught me more than a little, both about care and its contexts. Carol and Beth have been mentioned in earlier dedications, so I hereby dedicate this book to my son, Christopher, who, because it was late in coming, gets the whole dedication to himself.

D.S.B.

Introduction

It is my thesis that there is a moral context to all acts of care. This is true even of those acts of care which take the form of professional counseling and psychotherapy. It is important for both the counseling minister and the secular psychotherapist to recognize this truth. It is important for the minister because it is his primary task to provide this moral context as a *background* to his pastoral care and counseling. This is true even though at times he may temporarily relax the demands of this moral context in the specific situation of caring for another person. It is good also for the secular psychotherapist to recognize the validity of this assertion. Secular counselors or psychotherapists generally try not to become moralistic or advocate their own ethical standards in the process of working with clients. Yet it is becoming increasingly acknowledged that secular therapists assume a moral context—a more or less mutually recognizable and shared moral world that extends beyond the therapeutic situation and provides a moral horizon to the therapy even though it may not be directly invoked by therapists in the process of counseling.

The major difference between the minister and the secular psychotherapist is that the minister has a direct professional responsibility to help shape this moral universe of values and meanings. Whatever pastoral care and counseling he does must proceed within a context of this central professional obligation. The secular therapist does not have, as a part of his professional obligation, the task of forming and maintaining the larger moral universe of the society in which he functions. He may do this as a private person, but as a professional he has not been trained to occupy the role of a social moralist.

Most psychiatrists, psychologists, and social workers would agree with this view of their role. Yet they would also agree that there are many exceptions to this general rule. Many secular psychotherapists do take on the role of social moralists and use their professional expertise as sanction for their personal views. On the other hand, many ministers are becoming confused about their role as shapers of values and maintainers of meanings. They are aspiring to fashion their ministry more and more according to the model of the secular psychotherapist.

This only means that the distinction which I am drawing between the minister and the professional counselor is difficult to maintain in our present confused social situation. The goal of these chapters is not to yield to this confusion but to find a more adequate conceptuality which will set the situation more in order.

Part of the confusion about the boundary line between pastoral care and secular counseling comes about because of a rather simplistic view, held by many persons, about the scientific character of secular psychotherapies. The secular psychotherapies are not neutral scientific formulas for curing people. This is not to say that these disciplines in no way contain scientific knowledge. It does mean, however, that no matter how scientific is the theory behind various secular psychotherapeutic disciplines, the actual practice of psychotherapy is always a practical human art. In actual practice both the theory and the techniques of psychotherapy become absorbed into broader spheres of cultural meaning and the neutral scientific meaning is lost. This is why some psychotherapies, in their theory and practice, appear to be countercultural or downright anticultural while other therapies seem to help troubled individuals to conform to customary social and cultural expectations.

Most psychotherapists would like to assume the stance of moral neutrality and leave to the minister, philosopher, or poet the task of projecting society's normative values and standards of conduct. The very nature of psychotherapy, however, makes this difficult. Psychotherapy attempts to help persons with their pain and suffering. It aspires to help individuals to change the course of their lives and to grow. It frequently holds out images of cure. Insofar as it tries to move people from some state of unhappiness and distress to a new state of happiness or well-being, psychotherapy has native parallels to the dynamics of religion. Therefore psychotherapy, no matter how secular it is, easily becomes suggestive to the religious imagination. Sometimes the theory and practice of various schools of secular psychotherapy take on almost religious meaning both to their clients and to the larger literate public. Psychoanalysis, Jungian psychotherapy, Bernean, Rogerian, and gestalt psychotherapy clearly have taken on for certain segments of the public a quasi-religious meaning. When this happens, the theories and techniques of these therapies become inflated into encompassing orientations to life that function very much as do religious myths. They offer highly generalized interpretations about the purpose of life, the origin of human difficulties, and the secret for human change and betterment. When this happens, the psychotherapies become competitors with established religious orientations. They also become candidates for evaluation from the perspective of a critical philosophy of religion.

THE POINT OF VIEW

It is important to know where I stand—both professionally and as a human being—as I approach these lectures. By profession, I am a teacher in an interdenominational divinity school connected with a midwestern university basically dedicated to graduate research. Some people would call me a theologian. To some extent this is true, but there is a more specific way in which I think about my work. To say it simply, I like to discern the meaning and sense of religious claims, both the claims of so-called official religion and the claims of quasi religions. To approach religious material in this manner is basically a philosophical enterprise. I am interested not only to ask what a particular religious phenomenon means, I am concerned also to ask in what way the claims of a religious phenomenon can be considered as good and true. The traditional philosophical disciplines have been the major bearers of these questions until the recent past. Today, questions about the good and the true are pursued by a variety of disciplines; in fact, this basically philosophical task can proceed best if it takes place as an interdisciplinary inquiry. An interdisciplinary approach to broad philosophical issues necessitates, however, that one have a clear picture of the logic, powers, and limitations of the various disciplines that one is using. In these chapters, I will be conducting a kind of philosophical inquiry—in the broad sense of the word—into the significance and potential fruitfulness of the Christian tradition of pastoral care.

These chapters border on what is traditionally known as pastoral and practical theology. In the past, practical theology generally has been assigned a broader meaning than pastoral theology. Usually, practical theology refers to the reflective process which the church pursues in its efforts to articulate the theological grounds of practical living in a variety of areas such as work, sexuality, marriage, youth, aging, and death. Pastoral theology is narrower. It refers to the theological rationales used to undergird those ministries most specifically related to the guidance and care of persons—what is often referred to in the classical literature as the cure of souls or *cura animarum*. In my own work I take a more philosophical attitude to these subjects than is usually the case in either practical or pastoral theology. I am convinced that we are no longer in a cultural and social context that will permit us, with integrity, to use uncritically the symbols of our inherited religious traditions as revealed truths that only need to be applied adequately to particular concrete situations. And whether or not the cultural situation will permit it, it is certainly the case that such a procedure is impossible in the context of the open search for truth as this should proceed within a university—the locus of my work. Therefore, it is my goal both to interpret and to give some philosophical evaluation to what I consider to be the essence of the Christian tradition of pastoral care.

CARE AND THE SCRIBES AND PHARISEES

In the chapters that follow, we will discover an important dimension of care that Christians have almost forgotten. Not only is care to be associated with love, forgiveness, and grace; care in a Christian context also should exhibit a kind of practical moral inquiry into the way life should be ordered. In what follows, I will be resurrecting the ancient Hebrew images of the sage, the scribe, and the Pharisee. I will argue that we cannot understand Christian pastoral care unless we understand its Jewish backgrounds. When we do this, we discover that the cure of souls in ancient Judaism proceeded within a context of practical moral inquiry into the covenant responsibility of individuals. It is precisely this style of practical moral inquiry (midrash) which has been lost in the pastoral care of modern—especially Protestant—Christianity. We have learned from modern psychotherapy that we must not moralize, and that we should educe from the troubled person the initiatives and value framework needed to improve that individual. We have learned that lesson well, and it was an important lesson to master. But we now need to rediscover the ancient context in which to place our nonmoralistic attitudes. We need to learn that we can afford the luxury of not moralizing only when we have already developed a relatively firm moral outlook which both the helper and the person being helped can affirm. Only when our pastoral care contains within it dimensions of practical moral inquiry do we earn the right temporarily to relax these moral concerns and concentrate specifically on the emotional difficulties and the unique feelings of the person for whom we care.

To put it more directly, we have to know what we believe about the meaning of marriage as an important background to caring for people with marital problems. We must have a theological ethics of sexuality as a context for our work with persons with sexual difficulties. We must have something like a positive theology of interpersonal relations, death, illness, and aging before we can successfully care for and counsel persons undergoing crises in these areas of life. This is not to imply that our practical theologies about these areas of life are arrived at independently of our actual experience of working with people; certainly our theologies are directly informed by our actual involvement with individuals in need. I am suggesting, however, that too often we get the idea that caring for someone is primarily a matter of having the right emotional attitude and a little psychological knowledge. We often minimize the importance of the frameworks of meaning that we bring to our care. The difference between pastoral care and secular counseling is that the pastor's frameworks of meaning about various dimensions of life should be clear and obvious both to the general public and to the people who come for help in times of need. The secular helping disciplines generally try to play down the positive meaning frameworks about life and its various dimensions which they bring to the care that they exercise. Hence, ministers—whether pastors of congregations or pastoral counseling specialists—carry a larger burden and finally, I might add, a more important one. One motive for sharing these lectures with a larger reading public is my conviction that too many ministers and pastoral counseling specialists are failing to recognize this truth. Both are envying and imitating a bit too much the tidy focus and apparent expertise of the secular counselor and psychotherapist. Because the ministers and theological students who have heard these lectures felt encouraged and somewhat clearer about their central task, I bring them to a wider public.

I

The Contexts of Care

In what context is that helping activity generally referred to as "pastoral care" carried out? Most specifically I am addressing the context of pastoral care in the contemporary, mainline Protestant churches. My question is motivated by the suspicion that there is something problematic about this context. I suspect that there is a costly ambiguity in the minds of most pastors in such churches between the personal goals and the social-ethical goals that govern the context of pastoral care. This leads me to hazard the hypothesis that most pastoral care in the mainline churches is practiced without a great deal of sensitivity to the relation between personal problems and larger social-ethical questions. On the other hand, the reverse is probably also true. Social-ethical problems are often addressed without much knowledge of and sympathy for the more intimate and personal dimensions of human suffering. The practices of pastoral care are impaled on the dilemma between private and public that affects so many other enterprises in contemporary society.

There has been little in the recent literature of Protestant pastoral care which acknowledges that it has a larger context which somehow or other governs its specific goals and procedures. In fact, the reverse impression is often conveyed. The free and ready utilization by modern pastoral care and counseling of the diverse therapies and personality theories of secular psychology leaves the impression that larger ecclesiastical and cultural contexts are somehow neutral concerning its assumptions and procedures. The naïve attitude which believes that what gets results in one context can be readily appropriated by another seems to be all too prevalent among certain leaders in the main-line churches. Insights from psychoanalysis, from the therapies of Carl Rogers, Eric Berne, Fritz Perls, and B. F. Skinner, can be readily borrowed and employed with breathtaking rapidity. Group approaches, individual approaches, depth approaches, marathon techniques, encounter experiences, and sensitivity training have been quickly adopted and almost as handily discarded within recent years by both pastoral counseling specialists and many ministers in the parish. What is astounding about this phenomenon is not so much the willingness to experiment but rather the almost total lack of critical reflection on the question of compatibility. How do these various techniques and theories relate to the larger goals implicit in the church's ministry, its image of man and society, and its interpretation of history and life? Nothing more clearly indicates the church's lack of direction and general identity confusion than this penchant for borrowing uncritically and with almost reckless enthusiasm the newest technique that attracts the attention of the popular mind.

THE MEANING OF CONTEXT

The word "context" has a broad meaning. We need to specify its importance for pastoral care more carefully. To say that pastoral care has a context is to say that it takes place in a community known as the church with larger goals, characteristic styles, preferred means, and specifiable relations with other institutions as well as with the larger society of which it is a part. The goals, characteristic styles, and preferred techniques of pastoral care should in some way reflect and implement the goals of the group life of the larger church. On the other hand, the church and its methods of care also take place in a larger society with specifiable cultural goals, characteristic styles, and preferred methodologies of institutional and technological achievement.

In the parlance of contemporary systems theory, it can be said that pastoral care is a subsystem of the church and that the church, in some sense, is a subsystem of the larger society. Ideally there should be a continuity, although not necessarily a perfect one, between the goals and procedures of the church and the goals and procedures of pastoral care. Since we live in a highly differentiated and pluralistic society, the relationship between that system called the church and the various systems of contemporary society will be far more complex. Most of us would agree that, from its own perspective, the relationship of the church to the larger society must be one of critical and creative tension.

To say that pastoral care is somehow a subsystem of the church is not to suggest that its goals and methods cannot be informed by the goals and methods of the secular systems of care of the larger society. A great deal of borrowing from these secular disciplines has occurred in recent years. I do not want to criticize this process as such. But if the profession of pastoral care wants to maintain its identity, it must be able to demonstrate how its principles of selection are internal to the group identity of the church. Pastoral care and counseling must be able to show what is "Christian" and "pastoral" about what the minister—or the pastoral specialist—does when he offers his services. And pastoral care must be able to show that what it has borrowed from other disciplines will not corrupt the essential thrust of its own unique perspective.

To say that pastoral care is a subsystem of the church is not to say that it gets all its goals and procedures from the larger body. The unique experiences of caring for people in moments of crisis and conflict have themselves contributed to the larger self-understanding of the church, as it does even in our time. The identity of the group as a whole synthesizes and gives overall definiteness to the experiences of its various subfunctions. At best, the total identity of the church should articulate its personal, societal, cultural, historical, and transhistorical goals. Those subsystems of the church which are uniquely attentive to the personal, as is the case with pastoral care, both gain from and contribute to the self-definition of the other subsystems as well as the summary definition of the whole. There always have been varying degrees of tension between the different functions and systems of the church. For that matter there is always some conflict between the individual and social goals of any institution. But for various reasons, both good and bad, pastoral care functions have been of crucial importance for the self-definition of the modern mainline Protestant church. After only a brief interruption during the 1960's, they may be gaining increasing ascendancy in that church's self-understanding.

THE SPECIFIC CONCERNS OF PASTORAL CARE

What, then, are the specific concerns of the ministry of pastoral care in the church? The kind of definition I want to give is not a normative or theological definition. It is more nearly a historical and sociological definition. It attempts to describe the kinds of activities the church has performed for persons and called pastoral care. Seen in this fashion, pastoral care deals with what ministers have done to promote two principal functions: (1) the incorporation of members and their discipline in the group goals and practices of the church, and (2) the assistance of persons in handling certain crises and conflicts having to do with existential, developmental, interpersonal, and social strains. Suffice it to say that pastoral care in more recent times has had more to do with the latter goal than the former. When viewed from the perspective of seminary curricula, pastoral care in the last two decades has generally been narrowed to mean pastoral counseling. It has had to do with how pastors counsel people to handle existential, developmental, and interpersonal crises and conflicts. Social systemic conflicts primarily have been handled in pastoral care courses from the perspective of how they place certain personal and interpersonal strains on a person's private life. Courses in pastoral care and counseling in recent times have seldom dealt with the first historical goal mentioned above, i.e., how people are incorporated into and disciplined in the principal goals of the church. Pastoral counselors have seemed remarkably oblivious to this particular goal of *cura animarum* (the care of souls). They have been noticeably reluctant to bother about what these goals are or what they might practically mean for the pastoral care of the church.

This tendency to slight pastoral care as incorporation and equate it with pastoral counseling is not just a small oversight of interest only to ministers, vigorous laymen, and church bureaucrats. This shift signals a profound change in the religiocultural functions that the mainline churches have been playing in contemporary society. It suggests that these churches are giving up earlier efforts to socialize their members into a distinctive style of life. These churches are renouncing disciplines of change and nurture that might induce and maintain significant alterations in the behavior and attitudes of their members. Pastoral care is now more readily seen as something done by ministers to help people in a situation of emotional conflict and crisis. The shift probably reflects the situation of class, ethnic, and professional pluralism in an increasingly secular society. It may also reflect the accompanying tendency for people to come to churches not for ethical direction and a change of life-style but for social affirmation and for emotional and spiritual comfort.

Hence, in modern times, pastoral care has tended to focus on the important but limited functions of pastoral counseling. In addition, it has attempted to elaborate a rationale for its practice in a vacuum—without a sufficiently sophisticated theory as to *context*. On the whole, recent theory and practice of pastoral care has been without an ecclesiology, without an interpretation of modern cultural and institutional life, and without a social ethic.

When attention to these matters is neglected, much that passes for pastoral care in the Protestant church has an almost comic character about it. Images come to mind of ministers running off to seminars or workshops. They gain somewhat superficial doses of Rogers, Freud, Perls, or Berne and bring them home to try them out on needy, trusting, but often bewildered and then angry laymen. Many of these ministers are now confused about the church as a place where these highly stimulating techniques can be used. Some ministers conclude that there is something seriously wrong with the church and its people since they show a lack of interest in these therapeutic tools, which seem so manifestly beneficial. It seldom occurs to them that the problem may be in the tools themselves, in the uncritical transfer of them from one context to another, or both.

There is also something incongruous about the endless soul-searching and identity crisis of the so-called specialized pastoral counselors. In addition to their professional ministerial education, many of them are equipped with years of highly specialized training in one or more schools of psychotherapy. Most of them practice their arts in special centers physically removed from the setting and life of the local church. What they do in their therapeutic sessions is widely acknowledged among themselves to be almost indistinguishable from what goes on in secular counseling. Some—although by no means all—of these pastoral counseling specialists refer to themselves as "pastoral psychotherapists." They appear to mean that they are psychotherapists who are also Christians. It appears, however, that the fact that they are Christian has nothing special to do with the fact that they are psychotherapists. Thus there is lacking anything like an adequate explanation for the creation of a new profession of specialized pastoral counselors.

With considerable interest I have watched the leaders of the specialized pastoral counseling movement scramble for accreditation with various private and public health insurance plans. Such accreditation would add greatly to the public legitimation of specialized pastoral counseling, not to mention the financial benefits that such recognition almost automatically confers on the profession. But to receive this level of public verification presents the movement with a severe identity crisis. On the one hand, these specialists must demonstrate that as pastors they are not narrowly provincial, evangelistic, or confessional. Yet to build the case that they have something to offer not already found in the established helping professions, they have to demonstrate what is unique about their services.

This situation injects ambiguity not only into the specialized pastoral counseling movement but also into the life of the Protestant church and the local minister. Why is this so? In Western society most everyone seeks knowledge from experts. Thus the church is tempted to turn for consultation to the pastoral specialist. When it does so it learns that he is developing models and practices for a vastly different context and for vastly different purposes than is the pastoral care in the rest of the church. It is not clear how the leaders of the specialized pastoral counseling movement are seeking to balance this ambiguity.

THE IMPACT OF MODERN PASTORAL CARE ON THE CHURCH

All of the foregoing suggests a hypothesis that I now want to propose and to some extent support. The hypothesis is this: the impact of contemporary theories of pastoral care and counseling on the self-definition of the church has been ambiguous because of a lack of attention to questions of context. In discussing this hypothesis, I will leave many important theological and philosophical questions unanswered. My goal is to outline the contemporary situation with regard to our theories of pastoral counseling and care.

I want to set forth a series of propositions, any one of which demands more discussion than space will permit.

1. *The major contextual fact facing both the church and its pastoral care is the modern commitment to technological rationalization.* For our purposes, technological rationalization can be interpreted as a cultural commitment—possibly the principal cultural commitment characteristic of Western societies—toward improving the material standard of living by the application of modern methods of efficiency and scientific control.

Technological rationalization gives birth to the two children: pluralism and rapid social change. It must be admitted that this pluralism, especially in the United States, is partially due to population migrations. But at a deeper level it is the nature of a technological society to generate a diversity in occupations. Different occupational subgroups develop different interests and

goals depending on their position in society and the values that
govern their specific and immediate pursuits.[1]

In addition, cultural commitment to efficiency, scientific in-
ventiveness, and control gives rise to rapid social change. Rapid
social change puts enormous strain on the normative order of a
society.[2] New inventions and new institutional arrangements for
the sake of efficiency constantly give birth to novel enterprises
that need ordering and direction but that do not readily fit into
existing normative guidelines. When the rapid introduction of
technological innovations is a major characteristic of a society,
the normative order of both the larger society as well as the
church can never quite keep up.

Examples are easy to find. Our normative theories of the family in Western society have never caught up with the shock and
strains that the automobile unleashed upon it several decades ago.
Our standard theories of marriage and relationships between the
sexes have only recently begun to be rethought in the light of the
introduction of modern technologies of birth control. New possibilities in medicine in the area of organ transplants, the prolon-
gation of life, and the chemical and electrical control of the brain
are presenting traditional cultural and religious points of view
with new occasions for revision. I could list indefinitely the kinds
of issues that are likely to challenge our normative cultural system in the future. Never before has a society been forced to review
so critically and revise so rapidly its own moral traditions in the
face of rapid technological innovation. How resilient will Western
society be in successively altering and reconsolidating its normative cultural order to handle the myriad strains that our technological society will place upon it?

In the United States, dislocations of rapid social change are
further aggravated by the entrepreneurial activities of a basically
capitalistic economic system. This is not to say that rationalization, rapid social change, and pluralism are not prevalent in
socialist countries as well. The dislocations they produce, however, are perhaps more intense in capitalist countries.

This demand for a perpetually revised, normative cultural

order which now occurs in Western society presents a challenging situation for pastoral care. At a time when moral clarification is most needed because normative cultural values are in a state of crisis, pastoral care and counseling have, for the most part, abandoned the task of moral guidance. It has centered its activity on counseling, the analysis and correction of the emotional dynamics of troubled persons. Hence, much of the literature of pastoral care for the mainline Protestant churches has advocated a type of eductive counseling.[3] Eductive counseling attempts to clarify and reshape the emotional responses of a troubled person within the value framework which that person brings to the counseling situation.[4] Eductive counseling does not impose solutions on the person needing help; it tries to educe solutions, both emotional and moral, from the individual seeking counseling. Whatever the virtues of eductive counseling as a model for pastoral care (and there are many), its overemphasis signals a default on the part of the Protestant community. It is unwilling to tackle the hard problems of reconstructing the normative moral and cultural value symbols by which the church and its members should live. When the spirit of eductive counseling pervades the church, the tough value issues are left up to the individual's tastes and preferences. The church and the minister can properly address only the interpersonal and emotional dynamics.

This is precisely the issue that Karl Menninger raises in his book *Whatever Became of Sin?* Menninger is suggesting that if the church is no longer confronting issues related to the normative value symbols that inform the decisions of everyday life, then neither psychiatry nor pastoral care (nor any of the other helping professions) will have a moral context in which to focus on emotional and interpersonal dynamics.[5] Menninger's observations are based on the assumption that psychological problems involve value confusions just as frequently as they involve straightforward emotional and interpersonal dynamics. The thrust of Menninger's book is that there can be no care, by either the pastor or the psychiatrist, without balanced attention to *both* value issues and emotional-interpersonal dynamics. Implicit in Menninger and explicit in these chapters is the idea that the minister must necessarily work out of a context where clarification and stabilization of value issues is more prominent than the issues of emotional and interpersonal dynamics. On the other hand, the psychiatrist and the other secular helping professions must make emotional and interpersonal dynamics somewhat more the focus of their work than clarifying, revising, and stabilizing the value symbols that govern the various aspects of everyday life. Obviously, these differences of focus are luxuries that psychiatry and ministry can each afford only if the other profession is doing its task. Neither can ever rid itself of some accountability for both the moral and dynamic poles of care. However, both ministry and psychiatry must continue to respect and value the special focus of the other.

Much current controversy in pastoral care circles arises because they address issues that pertain to the emotional and interpersonal dimensions of care and all but ignore the normative value issues. The current preoccupation among both ministers and pastoral specialists as to which of the new psychotherapies is the best demonstrates the overidentification of pastoral work with the psychiatric pole of care. Whether gestalt psychotherapy is better than psychoanalysis, whether transactional analysis is more potent than the intrapsychic points of view of Rogers, Freud, and Jung—such preoccupations are with the "dynamic" issues of care. Fearful of being charged with moralism—a truly valid worry—pastoral care has abandoned explicit discussion about the goals, techniques, and proper limitations of the moral guidance tasks. How to enter into sensitive moral inquiry with troubled and confused individuals without becoming moralistic is, I contend, the major technical and methodological task for training in pastoral care in the future.

2. *Rationalization, rapid social change, and pluralism also tend to give rise to privatism and pietism, or what one might call the split between private and public values.* In situations of rapid social dislocation, people become exasperated by the challenges to the public social order and repeatedly sink back into nourishing pri-

vate values. As novel social arrangements appear and new technical procedures are unleashed requiring new normative guidelines, issues become unbelievably complex. Procedures for influencing the normative order of society become so diffuse that people give up in despair. They content themselves with ordering that aspect of their lives which appears to be still under their control—that is, their own personal and familiar existence.

The split between private existence and public policy is, at least in part, a result of social complexity. In more primitive societies this dichotomy, although never completely absent, was less accentuated. The split between private and public values is doubtless a worldwide phenomenon in advanced civilizations with urban cultures.[6] When things move beyond a certain level of complexity, people tend to lose track of what is happening. Unless they are specifically trained and deliberately provided with reliable information, they sink back into pietistic and private modes of existence.

This development has important implications for pastoral care. When pastoral care relinquishes the attempt to reestablish, at the level of the individual, a sense for normative values that might be shared by a general public, it is furthering the process of privatism and pietism. An ethos which suggests that moral values are to be bracketed and relegated to the private tastes of the individuals involved makes one more contribution to the general idea that there is no shared or public moral universe. In that case, secular individualism becomes the predominant style of the day.

3. *Certain secular practices of psychotherapy have been of crucial importance for pastoral care in recent times. They have greatly influenced and to some extent altered the ascetic-rational image of man traditionally associated with popular Protestantism.* In making this proposition, I am assuming the general validity of Max Weber's Protestant ethic hypothesis. This hypothesis suggests that the Lutheran doctrine of vocation and the Calvinist doctrine of predestination helped create a certain style of life which Weber called ascetic rationalism. What does ascetic rationalism mean

and how did classic Protestantism help create it?

Only a brief explanation is in order here. Max Weber, the great German economist and sociologist of religion, was keenly interested in the forces that brought about modern capitalism. Weber assumed that the unique feature of modern capitalism was the long-term organization of human energies toward a lifetime of rational and systematic behavior in an effort to create profit. How was such motivation brought about?

Weber believed he could demonstrate that capitalism thrived in those countries which were influenced primarily by the Protestant Reformation. The long-term motivation that he believed to be fundamental to capitalism was created by powerful religiocultural ideas put forth by Luther and Calvin. Weber believed that Luther's basic contribution was the doctrine of vocation or calling *(Beruf)*.[7] This conveyed to the average man that it was important to take his secular vocation seriously, since it was his avenue for serving God and expressing his gratitude for God's forgiveness and justification. This set of ideas led people to a new diligence in their secular jobs, many of which were in profit-making industries of various kinds.

But the Lutheran doctrine of *Beruf* was not sufficient, according to Weber, to produce a lifetime of systematic and methodical activity in the pursuit of profit. Weber believed that another idea out of the theology of Calvin made the crucial difference. This was the doctrine of predestination.[8] This doctrine asserted that God, in his absolute sovereignty, elected some people to be saved and others to be damned. There was nothing that the individual could do himself to affect his salvation one way or the other. Such a doctrine was certain to produce a great deal of anxiety in the heart of the individual Christian. The crux of Weber's Protestant ethic hypothesis rests on a theory about how certain Reformed pastors went about giving pastoral advice to these anxious people. Weber shows evidence that some pastors guided their parishioners to believe that if they were being blessed with material abundance and profit in this world, that was a sign that they had been elected for salvation in the next.[9] Weber believed that this stimulated Christians to alleviate their anxiety about salvation by a lifetime of rationalized and systematic activity in an effort to create wealth—wealth not to be enjoyed but to be understood as a sign of one's salvation. In this way, Weber believes, the theology of the Protestant Reformation, mediated by pastoral care, created the ascetic-rational image of man that undergirded the establishment of modern capitalism.

What I have written here should not be construed as a disparagement of Reformation Protestantism. In fact, Weber's thesis is not so much about what Luther and Calvin officially taught as it is about *how* what they said was misunderstood by anxious pastors and lay people and misapplied to everyday life. Weber's contention was that history is often shaped by the misinterpreted ideas of great minds.

There are various evaluations of the Protestant ethic synthesis. For myself, I believe that there are philosophical grounds for giving it high marks for its inner-worldliness. It took vocational activity in this world seriously. It also emphasized a long-range orientation toward the future. On the other hand, it can be criticized for utilizing anxiety over one's salvation as the primary motivating force. This produced a driven quality to the action of our forefathers. And although systematic activity with a future goal in mind is important for human adaptation, the value of such action is greatly reduced when its overriding goal is to produce wealth as a sign of salvation.

Not all the action of all Protestants manifested the marks of the Protestant ethic as we have described it. There were important occasions when Protestants were faithful to the deeper meaning of the founders. Of special importance for our subject are certain aspects of Calvinism related to what James Luther Adams calls its "totalistic impulse."[10] We will try to purge the Protestant ethic of its economic distortions and attempt to uncover and rehabilitate some of its deeper intentions.

What is interesting to note, from the standpoint of pastoral care, is that the methods of care in the mainline Protestant denominations during the nineteenth century and the early twentieth century reflected the assumptive world of the Protestant ethic. Historical research clearly suggests that this was the case. During the eighteenth and nineteenth centuries, Methodist small-group meetings, as well as pastoral visitations and conversations especially in the Presbyterian and Baptist churches, generally reeked with the scent of Protestant moralism.[11]

However, it is even more important for our purposes to note that the Protestant ethic was not just confined to the churches. Methods of guidance outside the church, in schools and other institutions of the culture, were also permeated by this ethos. Max Weber, Talcott Parsons, and others have tried to demonstrate (and with some success, I believe) that the character of ascetic rationalism and the values of instrumental activism constituted the dominant center of much of American religiocultural ideology, not just in the churches, but in the wider culture.[12]

On the other hand, certain modern theories of counseling and psychotherapy have, on the whole, been a significant ideological force undermining the Protestant ethic synthesis both inside and outside the church. To this extent, some modern therapies have been, to a considerable extent, countercultural. They have spawned values and attitudes that have conflicted with the dominant values of ascetic rationalism and its secular counterpart—what Talcott Parsons calls "instrumental activism." Psychoanalysis, Jungian and Rogerian therapy, and now the conglomeration of therapies associated with the human potential movement have all in different ways given rise to values of expressiveness, spontaneity, feeling, and openness. In addition, the humanistic psychologies have especially been antimoralistic, antiascetic, and antirationalistic in their sensibilities and values.[13]

I do not mean that these various psychotherapeutic schools were always in their *practice* spawning countercultural adjustments. In fact, most likely this was not happening. I am referring primarily to their *official written literature.* Much of it engendered a vision of the human at variance with the vision in the Protestant ethic. Psychoanalysis may have been the exception to this trend. But even psychoanalysis was interpreted, perhaps not accurately, as antiascetic and antirationalistic.

One of the fundamental questions that cultural historians of the future must deal with is this: How did a culture primarily committed to the values of ascetic rationalism and instrumental activism give rise to therapies that, as far as their *official* ideologies are concerned, are in substantial contradiction to these dominant values? Countercultural values have been long in developing and have many sources. A goodly number of the so-called modern therapies have been among the sources.

These so-called modern therapies, as I have said, greatly influenced the pastoral care practices of the church. They, in turn, have greatly influenced the way the church tends to articulate its theological self-definition. Therapeutic theologies have arisen (I myself have contributed somewhat to them)[14] and ideas from psychotherapeutic and counseling ideologies have influenced noticeably the theologies of Daniel Day Williams, Gregory Baum, Thomas Oden, Paul Tillich, and many others.[15] Moreover, the modern therapies have joined forces with other cultural movements such as existentialism and neo-orthodoxy in criticizing the legal and cultural institutionalization of technological rationalization. There are enticing analogies between therapeutic doctrines of acceptance, neo-reformation concepts of justification by grace alone, and various existentialist doctrines of the person.

4. *It is not surprising that the modern psychotherapies have given rise to explicit ideologies somewhat at variance with the quasi-official Protestant ethic synthesis.*

Scholarly analyses of therapeutic rituals in various cultures reveal that therapeutic procedures almost invariably involve a period of "sanctioned retreat" from the major social structures and cultural values operative in the particular society in question. Talcott Parsons observed that most contemporary therapies are still, despite their official ideologies, in service to the Protestant ethic. Therapy gives a sanctioned retreat from the structural demands of the occupational world so that a person can have the leisure to reorganize his energies for a more successful reentry into this world—a world subject to the Protestant ethos.[16]

Parsons' work on the sociology of the helping professions tends to define mental health as the "capacity" to function.[17] But, according to Parsons, "functioning" always goes on in the context of social expectations about role performance. Roles always contain both a *value* dimension and a *task* dimension, i.e., certain value frameworks which the role assumes and certain tasks which the person in that role is expected to perform. When a person subscribes to the values connected with a given social role but does not have the emotional "capacity" to perform them, then society considers the person ill.[18] If the person did not subscribe to the values that the role entailed, then society would judge that person to be in some way deviant. If the person is emotionally ill, then society will grant a sanctioned retreat from the task expectations of his various roles. It is assumed that the value commitments associated with these roles are still appreciated both by the helping professions that serve the person and by the person himself. During the period of sanctioned retreat, the ill person receives treatment. A major social presupposition of this sanctioned retreat is that both the therapist and the patient are committed to bringing the person back to a state of capacity to fulfill his social responsibilities.

In Parsons' sociological world, the religiocultural orientation that defines the value dimensions of roles in Western society is the Protestant ethic.[19] The sanctioned retreat received by the emotionally disabled person was *from* the public world of the Protestant ethic and the return was always *to* the public world of the Protestant ethic. Hence, for Parsons, the entire process of becoming emotionally disabled and receiving psychological treatment takes place in a religiocultural context, which, in the case of the United States, is the Protestant ethic. Therefore, according to Parsons, even secular psychological counseling is fundamentally a religious process and controlled by religious meanings.[20]

Parsons' thesis is probably true. Most secular counseling, psychotherapy, and psychological treatment may have operated in the way he describes. This would have been the case until recently, when we have witnessed the veritable explosion of psychotherapeutic schools and the appearance of a wide variety of goals for the therapeutic process. Parsons' description probably fits rather well most actual counseling and therapy, especially school and industrial counseling, adjustment counseling of all kinds, institutionally based psychiatric therapies, psychiatric social work, and social casework.

Parsons' thesis is also helpful for locating the sociological significance of certain features of most counseling and psychotherapy. Talk about the internal therapeutic process as being permissive, as exhibiting unconditional positive regard and acceptance, as not being moralistic and judgmental, as prizing all the feelings of the patient, and as accepting negative attitudes, would be understood from his perspective as having to do with transitional techniques and attitudes employed by the counselor to create the sanctioned retreat needed for the patient to analyze himself and reorganize his inner life.[21] They were temporary expedients designed to get the patient to relax long enough to explore his unhappiness or incapacity. Eventually the counselor would begin gradually to help the client reorganize his energies so that he could better cope with his Protestant world from which he had received his sanctioned vacation.

What Parsons has overlooked, however, in his comments on contemporary counseling and psychotherapeutic practices is the official rhetoric and ideologies that go along with them. At the level of actual practice, he may be close to the truth. At the level of the written literature of various psychotherapeutic movements, the story may be much more complex. There can be little doubt that the theories of personality, the conceptions of the counseling process, and certainly the official ideology of several of the new psychotherapies—especially the humanistic ones—entail value assumptions that are in considerable conflict with cultural Protestantism.

LIMINALITY AND THE THERAPIES

I have said that it is not surprising that the modern psychotherapies have articulated values somewhat in contradiction to the dominant values of popular Protestant culture. Why do I say this? Modern therapies have tried systematically to analyze some of the components of helping acts that appear to make people get better. In the process, however, some of these theories have given disproportionate attention to certain features of all therapeutic acts—especially the feature that Victor Turner calls the "liminal phase" of therapeutic rituals.[22] Victor Turner has taken an anthropological approach to the study of therapeutic rituals in the context of primitive societies. His categories of analysis are illuminating and may show forth certain dimensions of all healing processes. At the same time, his analysis may expose some of the theoretical imbalances that characterize certain contemporary theories of psychotherapeutic change. Following the work of Arnold van Gennep, Turner argues that most primitive rituals can be divided into three phases—the phase of separation, the liminal phase, and the phase of reincorporation.[23] Liminality refers to a phase of transition, of being in transit from one state to another state. Although the three stages are phases of most ritual acts, they are also phases of therapeutic or healing rituals in particular.

In the phase of separation there is a divestment of former roles and processes of identification.[24] In the liminal phase, the subject is conducted into what Turner calls an "undifferentiated phase." Here the subject and other participants in the ritual enter into a kind of utopian equality.[25] Former roles, commitments, and values are abandoned and an aura of innocence and rebirth permeates the ritual context. But the last stage moves beyond the liminal phase.[26] The subject is now reincorporated into the life of the group—it is hoped with renewed vitality. At this stage, the basic commitments, tasks, and responsibilities of the group life become operative again in his life. The period of liminality was transitional and temporary; the subject was soon returned to the major responsibilities operative in the life of his community.

Turner makes an observation that will probably spark some new trends in religious research. He states that whereas in most primitive societies liminality was indeed considered as transitional and always led to reincorporation into the structural life of the group, in more complex urban societies liminality gradually became a central goal of religion.[27] The free, undifferentiated state became an end in itself and was conceived in some sense as basically inimical to the structures and public tasks of the larger social order. Turner does not tell us how this happened. Earlier I suggested a tentative hypothesis. I said that pietism arose when urban complexity grew to the place where the individual no longer felt able to participate in the ordering of the basic public structures of the group. Let me restate that hypothesis in the light of our remarks about liminality. Liminality becomes disconnected from structure when structure becomes too complicated, too threatening, or too inaccessible and most religious people feel unable to participate.

Turner has introduced into religious studies a two-dimensional understanding of sacrality. For Turner, the sacred is a floating and dialectical experience. At one moment it can be on the side of structure, culture, social institutions, world creation, and world maintenance. From this perspective, religion and the nature of the sacred can look very similar to the way the sacred has been defined sociologically by Durkheim, Radcliffe-Brown, Luckmann, and Berger; or culturally by Geertz, Fromm, and Erikson. When the sacred shifts toward the pole of liminality and undifferentiated community (what Turner calls "communitas"), then religion and the sacred look very much like definitions associated with thinkers such as Buber (I-Thou),[28] Bultmann (the existential "moment" or "event"),[29] the Pauline-Lutheran understanding of justification by faith, or various understandings of mystical experiences as a process of deautomatization and destructuring of ordinary consciousness (Arthur Deikman).[30]

Not only does Turner believe the sacred involves this dialectical movement between structure and communitas, he believes this twofold movement is absolutely necessary for the survival and health of any society. He writes:

> What is certain is that no society can function adequately without this dialectic. Exaggeration of structure may well lead to pathological manifestations of communitas outside or against "the law." Exagger-

ation of communitas, in certain religious or political movements of the leveling type, may be speedily followed by despotism, overbureaucratization, or other moves of structural rigidification.[31]

In later chapters, I will integrate this dialectical understanding of the sacred into an adaptive-evolutionary theory of religion. The sacred as structure and the sacred as liminality and communitas will be seen as two moments in the adaptive struggle to construct a sociocultural symbolic world and to destructure and re-create such a world. Adaptation, especially in quickly changing environments, requires this kind of dialectical process. Even though I affirm the place that liminality has in man's religious experience, I will continue to associate religion and the sacred primarily with the normative symbolic forms of a culture. These forms give it its sense of direction and help order its various institutional arrangements.

There is clearly a relationship between what Talcott Parsons has called a "sanctioned retreat" and what Victor Turner is calling the phase of "liminality" in a ritual therapeutic process. Therapeutic processes seem to call for and necessitate some kind of separation from a society's religiocultural values and their specific embodiment in social roles, tasks, and obligations. This suggests that any therapeutic process, be it religious or secular, has within it an antistructural moment to become disconnected from the total movement of the therapeutic ritual and become an end in itself. When therapeutic theories give central prominence to the values of openness, the "I-Thou" encounter, spontaneity, the immediacy of experiencing and feeling, as not only a transitional dimension but as a general end, then it may well be that liminality has been severed from structure. Certain humanistic psychologies come close to making this separation. Psychoanalysis and psychiatry, insofar as they hide behind the protection of the medical model, can easily approach the same plight. Whenever a therapy, in the name of the medical model, says that it is only interested in restoring health (the capacity to act) without being concerned with the question of the particular finite values which that action will serve, then that therapy is serving to further the split between liminality and structure.

There are various ways, then, that modern therapies, in terms of their theoretical formulations, can become caught at the exits of liminality. There may be some justification for this tendency, especially for those therapies self-consciously working with the medical model. But it can produce disaster if it undermines the age-old task of moral guidance. There can be little doubt that moral guidance must take vastly different forms in modern societies than it has taken in earlier societies. Nevertheless, the pastoral counselor must be just as interested in the value symbols that govern the social structures and social roles impinging on the troubled individual's life as he is in the sanctioned retreat so necessary for the restoration of that person's health.

This presents the supreme challenge facing the pastoral counselor in today's society. If he is to fulfill his traditional role as a mediator of religiocultural values, he must be as much a moral philosopher (or moral theologian) as he is an expert in the diagnosis of emotional and interpersonal dynamics. He must do this to fulfill his own destiny. In his pastoral care he must function as a moral philosopher, even if he is at odds with the major value symbols of his culture. Furthermore, he must do this for the sake of the secular counseling specialist who wants to attend primarily to the exploration of emotional and interpersonal dynamics which the "sanctioned retreat" and the "liminal phase" permit. This is necessary, for if there is no moral world from which to retreat and to which to return, then emotional and mental incapacity will only be followed by moral confusion. When a person is so confused morally as not to be able to act or to choose, this in itself will end eventually in emotional incapacity.

How the pastoral counselor can do this without returning to authoritarianism and moralism, without becoming idiosyncratic and purely personal in his moral philosophy, and without giving up his sensitivity to emotional and interpersonal dynamics, are issues I will investigate in later chapters.

II

Roots of Care:
In Judaism and Early Christianity

We have investigated some of the historical roots of modern systems of care. If Parsons is correct, the religiocultural ideas of the Protestant Reformation have helped form some of the governing images of the human that have guided both religious counseling and certain forms of secular counseling. We are limiting our remarks about religious guidance primarily to contemporary Protestant forms. But it is not unreasonable to suppose that Catholic and even Jewish guidance has also been affected by the same vision. The Protestant ethic synthesis has influenced broad sectors of American life. Sociologists readily admit that although both Catholics and Jews have continued to maintain many distinctive features of their religious life, the Protestant ethic and its secularized version of instrumental activism has, to varying degrees, profoundly affected the life of these two religious bodies.[1] It is therefore reasonable to assume that it has touched in some way the practices of religious guidance characteristic of these groups.

We have said that certain features of both Protestant pastoral care and secular forms of guidance had their roots in a cultural vision with distinctively religious dimensions. We called this religiocultural vision the Protestant ethic. When by the process of secularization the Protestant ethic is denuded of its specifically theological referents, it takes the form of instrumental activism —the idea that through systematic practical activity in the secular world one can improve the quality of life and solve some of its inequalities, deprivations, and irritations. This future-oriented, activistic, and somewhat heroic vision of life may have been the formative influence shaping our vision of the human and guiding both our general cultural life and our helping disciplines, be they religious or secular.

I now propose to go deeper and discuss some of the antecedents to the Protestant ethic synthesis. In these next chapters we will trace some of the relationships between religiocultural visions of the human and systems of guidance and care that have characterized Western culture. The purpose of this overview is to argue that there has always been a relationship between religiocultural visions and systems of care and guidance. I want to show some of these relationships and carry farther the idea that as this has been the case in past societies, it is also the case in our own, even though these relationships can be lost so easily from view in our kind of society.

In this broad historical sketch, I will occasionally refer to more ancient forms of care by the time-honored phrase of *cura animarum,* the cure of souls. Before the modern period, the problems of troubled persons were seen in a religious and spiritual context. They were thought to be primarily religious difficulties requiring the powers and expertise of specifically religious personages.

RELIGION AND THE CARE OF SOULS

Max Weber points out that at various times and in various religions during the history of man, the care of individual souls became the dominant interest of religion, usurping and in some ways undermining more corporate or social concerns.[2] This was not the case in the earliest forms of religion. Primitive religion, it appears, sees the individual in strong relationship to the group. Marcel Mauss, in his famous article entitled "A Category of the Human Spirit," has pointed out that in certain primitive religions the individual was subsumed under the tribe, role, and ancestral reincarnation that his name represented. His significance rested in his tribal role and his ancestral heritage rather than his individuality as such.[3]

Such a world was doubtless secure and unambiguous. Honor and responsibility were determined precisely for the individual by the group as a whole. Criminal and neurotic deviations were almost minimal in such a world. The religion of such a people generally was devoid of the themes of salvation typical of the great religions of civilization such as Christianity, Hinduism, Buddhism, or Islam.[4] Man's place in the world was well defined. His rewards were distributed more precisely and less accidentally. And if he hoped for a life after death, he believed it would come more as a natural inheritance of an honorable life on earth than as a result of a salvation to be achieved.

What happens when war or technological advancement break up such a world and such a religion with its communal solidarity and lack of individuality? Max Weber and other scholars believe that magicians, mystagogues, shamans, and witch doctors take on special significance.[5] They are healers, magicians, counselors, and sorcerers who meet the needs of individuals in ways that the larger, more public and communal cults either cannot or do not. It is not that such personages arise when primitive communal religion begins to break down. Certainly, the ecstatics, magicians, and shamans have been there always and played a part in these religions. But when the communal religion breaks down, their role is more enhanced and progressively more independent of the larger communal or tribal cults. Subcults, followers, disciples, and individual seekers begin to develop around these figures. And at the same time, it appears that the central communal cult, the public religion, fades in significance.[6]

It is not my intent to push the idea of a too-close relationship between the importance of individual healers or guides and the emergence of the so-called salvation religions which assert a unique interest in and concern with the welfare and salvation of the individual soul. My concern is, rather, to show that it is not unusual for ideologies and practices connected with *cura animarum* to have a crucial influence on a people's understanding of the nature and purpose of religion. And so it may be in our time. The so-called therapeutic theologies and the therapeutic understanding of the mission of the church in our time are turns that religions have gone through before. Whether they are good or bad depends on philosophical judgments of a kind that I am not prepared to pursue for the moment. Let us stay more descriptive and historical at least for a while.

There is considerable evidence that therapeutic interests and ideologies have great influence on the self-understanding of the contemporary church. There are some who suggest that pastoral care should be the primary task of the church. It has been a common understanding in much of contemporary sociology—especially in the work of Talcott Parsons[7]—that because of the extreme differentiation and relative autonomy of the public institutions of modern societies, the church's role in society has narrowed; its primary role is to assist families in socializing children into the primary religiocultural values of our society. This suggests that the church is primarily residential, has little access to and power over the values and norms of the public realm. Its main function is to socialize people into the best there is in the civil religion of a society.

When these sociological pronouncements filtered down to the leaders of the Protestant churches during the beginning of the 1960's there was a strong reaction. A series of important books, beginning with Gibson Winter's *The Suburban Captivity of the Churches*[8] and culminating with Harvey Cox's *The Secular City,*[9] began to call for a more aggressive role on the part of the church in the formation of public policy. This was an effort to restore official religion to its more active role as the shaper and the maintainer of the total corporate sphere, especially the value symbols that form its vision. Although it may be too early to say that this movement has passed completely, it is clear that the task is far more complicated than it was thought to be in 1965 when the movement was in its finest hour. It is clear that this thrust of the mid-1960's has waned and that mainline Protestant churches are renewing their interest in the care of souls. The care of souls as the central element of religion is once again prominent in a good deal of contemporary religious life.

MAGIC AND RATIONAL GUIDANCE
IN ANCIENT JUDAISM

What do we know about pastoral care (or *cura animarum*) in the history of Christianity? Several important works have come out in recent years. Certainly John McNeill's *A History of the Cure of Souls* is the all-time classic. William Clebsch and Charles Jaekle's *Pastoral Care in Historical Perspective* is a close second. In addition, there has been renewed interest in locating contemporary secular systems of guidance and therapy in a historical context—for instance, the work of Henri Ellenberger in *The Discovery of the Unconscious,* Jerome Frank in *Persuasion and Healing,* Ari Kiev in *Magic, Faith, and Healing,* Victor Turner in *The Ritual Process* and *The Drums of Affliction,* and Claude Lévi-Strauss in his *Structural Anthropology.*[10] Certain sociological views of the modern therapies have also helped us to gain a larger perspective on the role of modern systems of guidance in Western civilization. Important here is the work of Philip Rieff in *The Triumph of the Therapeutic,* Paul Halmos in *The Faith of the Counsellors,* and Kurt Back in *Beyond Words.*[11] There are many others. We are beginning to learn something about man's systems of moral, spiritual, and therapeutic guidance in their broadest manifestations. In addition, this makes it possible for us to learn something more specific, by comparison and contrast, about *cura animarum* in the history of Christianity and modern Protestantism. When read from a certain perspective, the brilliant sociological work of Max Weber is of special importance for this inquiry.

Before discussing the care of souls from the perspective of early Christianity, we need to know something about ancient Judaism as well. In making this rapid review, I do not mean to suggest that either the Old Testament or the New Testament is normative in any simple sense for either religious or secular guidance today. But it may be that this historical review will help us to find images of the human that will contribute to our own constructive efforts to develop a view adequate for guiding the helping disciplines today. A comparative perspective will be used when possible. Only then will some of the unique dimensions of both the Judeo-Christian heritage and modern practices become clear.

In general, the Jewish and Christian traditions of spiritual guidance have a far more prominent ethical dimension than most of our present-day literature in Protestant pastoral care would lead us to believe. Still living off the revival of neo-Reformation theology of the 1940's and 1950's, with its emphasis on God's love and salvation by *grace alone,* many contemporary theorists of Protestant pastoral care tend to be oblivious to the way the ethical demands of law and the will of God operated in Judaism and early Christianity. Grace and forgiveness mean something different for us in our anomic and normless age than they did for Jesus or for Paul, who both functioned out of the context of the Torah and its written and oral exposition.

It is important to remind ourselves that Christianity grew out of Judaism, and that Judaism was a distinctively ethical type of religion, a religion of inner-worldly asceticism. The phrase "inner-worldly asceticism" comes from Max Weber's sociology of religion. Its meaning varies somewhat, depending on the context in which Weber is using the phrase. In general it refers to a certain orientation to life, a certain strategy for handling the threats of evil and meaninglessness that always promise to engulf people wherever they are. Inner-worldly asceticism refers to an orientation of living that emphasizes a positive valuation of life in this world. It approaches this life with a type of practical rationality that actively orders and seeks mastery over impulse and action in an effort to make them conform to the guidelines of certain practical rules of behavior.[12] Inner-worldly asceticism can be contrasted with three other broad orientations to life which Weber thought characterized the strategies of the major world religions. Other-worldly (world-rejecting) asceticism tends to devalue life in this world and uses practical rules and ascetic disciplines actively to break or reject one's attachment to this life and achieve an existence in another, more perfect world.[13] Two other broad orientations discussed by Weber were inner-worldly and other-worldly mysticism. Inner-worldly mysticism entails a less active, less directed, more resigned and passive effort to achieve harmony with things in this life.[14] Other-worldly mysticism entails a less active, more resigned effort to gain unification with a realm that transcends the mundane world. In general, when Weber uses the word "ascetic" he means an active orientation to life that seeks to order impulse and needs by directive intention. Asceticism need not lead—although sometimes it does—to a rigid denial of self and of the good things of this life.[15]

Weber believed that ancient Judaism was a form of inner-worldly asceticism, but not the purest example.[16] Reformed Protestantism was for him the clearest example of inner-worldly asceticism, but the forces and motivations that brought about these similar orientations were somewhat different.[17] What is important for our purposes is that Weber believed that ancient Judaism was a distinctively ethical type of religion. By this he meant that ancient Judaism believed that human action was important for the transformation of this world.[18] The response of ancient Judaism to the experience of evil—the discontinuity between the ideal and the actual—was not flight, resignation, or the manipulation of inner responses. It was an ethical response which attempted to order human action to produce more congruence between the ideal and the actual, to produce more social justice and peace on earth. It sought to make social reality conform to the rules of action designed to implement the ideal society.

The Jewish religion grew out of a confederation of peasants and herdsmen who had banded together in a covenant (*berith*) to fight urban patricians and marauding bedouin. Their God was a mighty God of war who not only presided over their covenant with one another but who was actually a member of this covenant. The covenant was an exchange of obligations. For acceptance of Yahweh as God and obedience to his law, this mighty God would lead them to victory in war and grant them fruitfulness of progeny. Judaism, as Weber has pointed out, was a religion of a pariah people—a "guest" people—a people who were on the "outside," living on the land of urban patricians. They were subject to the pressures and injustices of "host" classes and castes more securely established than they.[19] In this way ancient Judaism can be strikingly contrasted with the other-worldly attitude of Hinduism and medieval Catholicism. Both Hinduism and Catholicism were religions of host or established groups and were used to integrate other outside groups, tribes, or aliens into the dominant religiocultural ethos.[20]

There were many types of holy men in ancient Israel—ecstatic war magicians such as Samuel, priests, prophets, wise men, and later, scribes and rabbis. For our purposes, it is good to distinguish between four classes—priests, prophets, wise men, and scribes. The priest, the wise man, and the scribe—each was, in different ways, a kind of *directeur de l'âme* ("director of the soul") in ancient Israel. And all of them more or less knew and assumed the Torah, the law.[21] Levitical priests were closest to the cultic activity of the confederacy and later of the royal house.[22] The cultic activity of the Levitical priests was designed primarily to implement and to expiate guilt when the covenant law was broken. Although there were important exceptions to this, the outstanding characteristic of the Levitical priestly groups (especially when compared to the Hindu Brahman or the Greek oracles) was the rational exposition of the covenant law—especially for individuals. This last point is so important and indicative of the richness of Weber for the clarification of the meaning of *cura animarum* in various historical contexts that I want to quote from him at length.

> In any event, the Levites did not gain their prestige by their training in the proffering of sacrifices for the community, but by training in purely rational knowledge of Yahwe's commandments, of ritualistic means to amend offenses against them by *chattat, asham,* fasts, or other means, and thereby ward off threatened misfortunes and to undo already incurred ones. This was of interest to the king and the community, but, above all, to private persons. With mounting politi-

cal pressure upon Israel, this very need increased generally. It became the sole meaning and intent of the Levitical Torah to satisfy this need by instruction of patrons. Instruction was given for hire (Micah 3:11). Sins were confessed to the Levite (Num. 5:6 f.) and he "reconciled" the guilty one with Yahwe (Lev. 4:20, 31; 5:10; 6:7). For the private client this was his most important service. The ascendency of this relatively rational, educative influence of the Levites—however primitive in content at first one may imagine their teaching—went hand in hand with the decline of the ancient ecstatic-irrational war prophets and Nebiim of the peasant militia.[23]

In fact, this became so important that in postexilic times the priestly expositors of the covenant law became more and more independent from the cultic practices and began to develop a distinct group of Torah experts, interpreters, and teachers. These became the scribes, teachers, and Pharisees of later Judaism. They were the practical expositors and teachers of the social-ethical laws of the Torah. In comparison to other religions, what is peculiar to them is their practical rationality—their lack of magical and mystical techniques, their interest in everyday behavior, and their closeness to the lives of the average man. These were the practitioners of pastoral care par excellence. Their handling of problems of guilt, anxiety, confusion, and forgiveness assumed a wealth of practical laws. Their primary tool was knowledge— not esoteric or mystical knowledge, not orgiastic or gnostic or secret wisdom—but rational knowledge of the law, its casuistry and everyday application.[24]

In later times, Pharisees supplemented the Torah with an oral tradition that extended its legal implications. The Pharisees (in contrast to the priestly Sadducees) were interested in a living Torah, a living law that was updated and made more applicable to the changing times. The oral tradition was the result of this impulse to take the Torah to the people, to make it possible for all Jews to live by the law, to make, in fact, the Jewish nation into a "nation of priests" cognizant and obedient to the law. The Pharisees were practical rationalists par excellence who were always attempting to be, at one and the same moment, faithful to the inherited tradition and yet diligent about extending it and modifying it to cover the novel circumstances that life always brings.[25] Study and rational disputation were their major tools.[26] Pharisaic Judaism constituted what safely can be called normative Judaism of the people at the time of Jesus' life.[27] In the second century A.D., the oral tradition finally was collected and written down in the Mishnah. The Talmud consists of the Mishnah and various commentaries that have been added.[28]

In addition to these groups, there were wise men. They were of ancient vintage and, although they knew and taught the law, they also had access to other strands of practical ancient wisdom from Egypt, Mesopotamia, and possibly Greece.[29] Scribes, on the other hand, probably emerged from the priestly groups and made their appearance as an independent group during the exile and the time of Ezra. Wise men were older and were probably separate from the priesthood from the beginning.[30]

Prophets too tended to assume and work with the law. But only accidentally did they become involved in the guidance of individuals.[31] Their primary concern was the destiny of the holy nation of Israel. They judged contemporary situations with regard to assessing man's faithfulness to the law of Yahweh. Yet they tended to interpret this law in ways that gave it new simplicity, vividness, and rigor.[32] Prophets simultaneously simplified and rigorized the law, whereas priests and scribes applied, complicated, routinized it. Max Weber has made the interesting observation that the closer priests and scribes get to the masses, the more likely that their handling of the law will develop magical and superstitious dimensions.[33] Magic is something that the masses seem to want. It promises quick solutions, wishes fulfilled, pain removed, rewards now, and this through the manipulation of both supernatural and mundane powers. Rational guidance is born out of and can quickly sink back into magic and sorcery. The emergence once again in Western society of sorcery, magic, rapid and miraculous cures in the areas of practical guidance is probably a sign that more rational or patterned systems of cultural or religious codes of conduct are collapsing. People resort to witch-

craft (as Anthony Wallace and others suggest) when more pre-
dictable, accessible, and manageable ways of obtaining life's de-
serts are not available to them.[34] The so-called legalism of Old
Testament religion is often contrasted with the emphasis on love,
forgiveness, and grace in the New Testament. But it should also
be contrasted to magic. In contrast to the solution of life's problems through magic, sorcery, and divination, Judaism more and
more emphasized a practical, this-worldly, ascetic, and ethical
rationalization of personal and public conduct.

CARE AND THE MINISTRY OF JESUS

Let us remind ourselves that systems of guidance in early
Christianity assume a positive Jewish ethos and culture with its
emphasis on the ordering of everyday life by a rational code of
practical law—a code that was thought to be the expressed will
of God. It is important to remember this, because we have hardly
anything like it in American culture today, especially among the
more affluent middle classes. Cultural codes for practical conduct
are diffuse. Most people consider such codes a matter of personal
taste. Others who feel more intensely about their assumed codes
have nothing like a Torah or Talmud—an inherited tradition that
is easily accessible, interpreted, rationally taught, and broadly
applicable to wide ranges of public and private life. The organization of practical conduct, except as it touches areas specifically
under the rule of the law of the state, is increasingly a matter of
individual taste and subjective preference. At the same time that
modern life has become more *rationalized* at the level of legal,
economic, and scientific pursuits, it has become *less rationalized*
at the level of practical social conduct pertaining to the areas of
family, interpersonal relations, sexuality, and recreation.

The significance of Jewish culture and law for primitive Christianity is to be seen first in the likely fact that Jesus himself was
to some extent a moral teacher very much in the tradition of the
scribes and Pharisees. His method of teaching individuals and
small groups and his knowledge of and concern for the law sug-

gest that this may be an accurate way of perceiving him. Critical
as he was of these groups, he often functioned similarly to them.
He was referred to frequently as "rabbi."[35] He came to fulfill the
law, not to abrogate it. There were ways in which he functioned
as a healer, but his healing was always subservient to and a sign
of his authority to proclaim the ethical demands of the will of
God and the coming of his kingdom on earth. In some ways he
operated as a prophet, but he did not have the prophet's concern
with the political fortunes of Israel. He was not preoccupied with
the political independence of the Jewish nation. But like some of
the prophets, he handled the law in such a way as to simplify it,
idealize it, and intensify the felt sense of the relationship between
the law and the will of God.

I have found it helpful in understanding Jesus to see him as
neither a legalist nor an antilegalist, but rather as a supralegalist.
This idea, developed by Erwin Goodenough in his *Psychology of
Religion,* is designed to describe the creative legalist—i.e., the
man who is imbued with a legal tradition but who, by virtue of
unexplained creative acts, simultaneously idealizes certain aspects of the tradition while simplifying or eliminating other aspects.[36] This is what Jesus did with the Jewish law. The formula
goes something like this: "You have heard other legal teachers,
fathers, even Moses himself, say to you that such and such are
the rules and laws for your conduct under God, but I say that
these are quite inadequate; the truth is that you should do even
better." In legalism, the letter of the law is sufficient; in supralegalism, the inner meaning, the deeper objective, the ideal direction of the law must become the guide. Jesus, Francis, Gandhi,
and possibly Luther, are all examples of the supralegalist.

The supralegalist produces a twofold effect in his followers. On
the one hand, there is a terrific sense of freedom because of the
simplification and elimination of an overly burdened system of
legal casuistry. On the other hand, the supralegalist holds out
nearly impossible visions of perfection which men sooner or later
despair of attaining. When the wider principles of the supralegalist begin to degenerate once again into legalism and the letter of

the law, one is often left with a new legalism that may be even more rigorous and complex than the one before.

It is important to realize that neither the historic Jesus nor the Christ of faith is represented as creating a moral code or law as such—not even an idealized one.[37] What we do have are "sayings" or hyperbolic pointers toward some impossible goal that are, in effect, like saying, "You have a moral obligation to do the impossible." Before these sayings, we are all guilty. We are not to commit murder, but we are also not to get angry at one another. We are not to commit adultery, but we are also not to have a wandering eye, not even a playful one. We are to cut off the offending member. Divorce is ruled out and we are in no way to resist our attackers. We are to forgive indefinitely. The church always has handled these sayings quite selectively, but yet it has attempted occasionally to abide by some of them—especially the ones on adultery and divorce.

The essence of these sayings was to point to a rather nonspecific vision of how moral thinking can rise above the customary, inherited codes of a particular cultural situation. They project the vision of a transmoral conscience—a conscience that can rise to a higher ethic than the specific moral code that governs the workaday world of man.[38] A dimension of the Christian kerygma seems to be the raising of this transmoral or supralegalist vision as a demand of a loving God—a God who was even then in their midst inaugurating a new age and bringing to an end the old.

It is important to understand the relationship between legalism and supralegalism. It is impossible to make a supralegalist statement without first assuming a legalist code. This is another way of saying that one cannot rise above legal codes unless one has them. One cannot transcend morality without first having a morality. There must be codes which guide everyday life before more ideal supralegal visions can be entertained. But the logical relationship between legal and supralegalist visions points to an ambiguity that affects cultures nourished by supralegalism. On the one hand, they are prone to legalize and codify their supralegal vision and come up with an impossible Puritanism or asceticism. On the other hand, they are likely to neglect their cultural codes and, in the name of their supralegalist vision, fade off into antinomian and amoral postures.

If my understanding of the relationship between legalism and supralegalism as it operated in the life of Jesus is correct, it follows that it is impossible for many who call themselves Christians to be supralegalists, to transcend the law and find its deeper intention. Why is this the case? The answer: Western society has nothing comparable—for the mass of its people—to a Torah, Midrash, Mishnah, or Talmud. The rapidity of social change has tended to undercut a working sense of cultural tradition about rules and patterns of conduct. The religiocultural value symbols in Western societies are increasingly more confused. In saying this, I do not want to convey the idea that the Torah and oral tradition at the time of Jesus were completely intact without any strain, confusion, and obsolescence whatsoever. But relatively speaking, primarily because of the casuistical work of the Pharisees, the fund of practical rules governing everyday behavior was reasonably firm and still taken seriously. We can hardly say this is the case for the broad mass of people in Western society today. Therefore our efforts to be supralegalists inevitably take the character of antinomianism. Certainly there are numerous dead and oppressive rules cluttering the moral landscape in our society. But to become preoccupied with divesting ourselves of these rules and the value symbols that accompany them is to miss the point. The issue is, rather, what will be the new rules and value symbols that will replace the old ones? Also, what will be the continuity between the old and the new, if any?

The failure to understand these truths points to the inadequacy of most so-called ideologies of liberation. Such present-day ideologies believe that the primary task is to rid ourselves of the dead and disfunctional rules and value symbols which are no longer adequate to the present social situation. These philosophies seem unable to recognize that the major task is to establish the rules which will guide us in our new situation. Liberation is only half of the truth and a dangerous half-truth at that. It fails to see that our problem is not ridding ourselves of legalism, but of modifying a dead legalism into a live moral tradition. Later I will argue further for this point of view. I will try to do so not just out of respect for the Judeo-Christian tradition but in order to show the necessity of a moral basis for human life, and the related need for rules to govern the myriad transactions of daily life.

CARE IN THE EARLY CHURCH

The ambiguity of legalism and supralegalism was not completely absent from the life of the early church. By and large, antinomian tendencies were rejected firmly and a mode of warm and spiritually vitalized discipline became the primary mode of pastoral care in the early church. It is important to remember that the early church was animated by a sense of the risen Christ. One cannot fail to be impressed by the personal warmth and principled concern for individuals that emerges in the Synoptic records and especially in the letters of Paul. This warmth and concern was buttressed by a rather clear continuing adherence to the noncultic aspects of the Jewish law. On the whole, cultic restrictions pertaining to food and circumcision were rejected. This prepared Christianity to become a universal religion and to overcome the cultic pariah status of the Jewish people. Yet the background of the Jewish law in the areas of social-ethical conduct lingered on as a measure of right conduct. The supralegalism of Jesus' sayings made it possible to dispense with the cultic aspects of the Jewish law. The command of Jesus for forgiveness made it possible for the early church to deal charitably with those who broke its standards of conduct and led it to assume that God would forgive as well. We are impressed, however, by the relative clarity of the early church's everyday codes of behavior. It had a capacity to discipline—even reject—offenders, and yet was ready to forgive and reinstate the offender when he was prepared to admit the errors of his ways and to change his conduct.[39]

On the basis of these brief observations, let me make a summary statement about the nature of early Christianity and its practical guidance for life in the church. To do this, however, I must restate some of the things that were said about Judaism. The basic symbols of the Jewish religion have to do with the symbols of covenant (*berith*) and promise of a pariah people, a guest people who had confederated to obtain a fuller life—land, progeny, herds, and food. The structure of existence suggested by these symbols of covenant and promise have two dimensions: (1) a future-oriented expectation of receiving something in this world either for oneself or for one's progeny which one does not have at present; and (2) a sense that the primary condition for realizing this expectation is obedience to the covenant law, which is understood and appropriated more or less rationally. In this context, guidance, care, or *cura animarum* (whatever we would like to call it) took the form of rational training and appropriation of the details of this covenant law which was being complexified constantly under the pressures of changing circumstances and casuistic application.

In postexilic times, the pattern of covenant and promise changed somewhat. The pattern of expectation had to do with the restoration of something that one had possessed briefly but had lost. This is still the expectation of a pariah people, a people on the outside, now either the prey of or dependent on foreign powers to the north. Secondly, this postexilic expectation was accompanied by an intensified sense that perfect obedience to the law was the primary condition for realizing this expectation.

In the early Christian community, the sense of promise and expectation shifted again. The roots of the Jewish sense of existence as a pariah people are still visible. But now the expectation of the coming of the kingdom is intensified. It is coming indeed and there are early signs that it is partially here already. Fulfilling the law is no longer a condition for the coming of the kingdom. Rather, now the law has been idealized and simplified. Obedience to it is a sign of whether an individual will participate in the kingdom when it does indeed fully arrive. In this context, pastoral care took the form of intense, warm and personally oriented instruction about this expectation, the deeper meaning of the law, and corporate efforts to discipline and forgive those who could not live by this new idealized law as a sign of their direct obedience to the will of God.

In short, Judaism and primitive Christianity are fed and energized by symbols of radical renewal and reversal designed to give a pariah people (people on the outside and people who have lost out) a hope for a reversal of their situation. The condition for this reversal (as it was in ancient Judaism) or the condition for participation in this reversal which inevitably was to take place (as it was in early Christianity) was obedience to a code of daily living (Torah and oral law) more or less rationally taught, appropriated, and applied.

If there is anything unique about *cura animarum* in primitive Christianity, it is the combination of spiritual warmth and a structured code of everyday ethical behavior. Pastoral care proceeded in a mode of ordered spirituality. It was an ordered spirituality placed within the context of the Jewish expectation for a future reversal of present agonies. This future hope, accompanied by a rational code of daily behavior, gets to the heart of what was happening in primitive Christianity.

We will look in more detail at this particular structure of human existence, this unique combination of future orientation and ordered spirituality—what John Cobb has referred to as "spiritual existence."[40] Christian existence, for Cobb, includes within it prophetic and Pharisaic elements. Prophetic existence was intense personal confrontation with and response to the direct will of God. Cobb believes that Pharisaic existence was the form that prophetic existence took during Jesus' day. Pharisaism combined intense ethical consciousness with a future hope. Yet Cobb believes that Pharisaic existence was devoid of a vivid awareness of the presence of God. Christian existence organizes the prophetic intense personal responsibility before God and the Pharisaic total ethical ordering of daily existence into a context empowered by the spiritual presence of God. It is clear that in primitive Christianity we have an image of hope and an image of the spiritual renewal of life. It is to these symbols of renewal that people who have called themselves Christians invariably appeal, even though their appeals have seldom matched the particular form these symbols of renewal took in the original community of those who saw themselves as followers of Christ. How modern believers may avail themselves of these symbols of renewal and the combination of spiritual warmth and ordered conduct which surrounded them—this will be discussed later.

III

Roots of Care:
In Christian History

The earliest substratum of Christian symbols is rooted in the inner-worldly ethical concerns of the ancient pariah people who formed a confederation to improve their lot on this earth, and who also grounded their life together in a covenant with their God and with one another. This covenant gave birth to a more or less rationally articulated system of legal codes that applied to a wide range of life and that gradually replaced—although never completely—the ordering of life's pursuits through appeals to magic. The ethical character of this cultural conglomerate was complicated somewhat in primitive Christianity, but by no means completely lost. Although the early Christian community was vitalized by a sense of the inbreaking of the spirit of God, the coming kingdom, and the return of Jesus, the rational-ethical ordering of life was still very much a part of their existence. However, during the later New Testament period, the seeds are sown for an other-worldly understanding of the future renewal or reversal—a view that is to emerge in full bloom at a later time.

What I am arguing is something easily lost sight of today—i.e., the overall ethical character of this Hebrew and early Christian cultural conglomerate. The basic symbolism of this conglomerate is inner-worldly, ethical, and ascetic. This is in contrast to certain other broad ways of characterizing the major world religions developed by Max Weber—i.e., other-worldly asceticism, other-worldly mysticism, and inner-worldly mysticism. It is important to say this, especially in our present situation. We are tempted to reject certain modern distortions of inner-worldly asceticism in the name of various forms of inner-worldly and other-worldly mysticism.

In view of these remarks, let me state a major thesis: Because of our disillusionment with certain distortions (primarily economic) of the ethic of Protestant inner-worldly asceticism, we are tempted to repudiate the ethical and ascetic dimensions of the central thrust of the Judeo-Christian tradition and substitute in its place various forms of inner-worldly or other-worldly mysticism. As a corollary, I will argue that the secular therapies and their influence on the pastoral care practices of the church may be one of the primary avenues through which these mysticisms will emerge. I will further contend for a rehabilitation of this tradition of inner-worldly ethical asceticism by cleansing it of certain economic distortions that characterized part of its history in modern times.

Before characterizing the religiocultural context of care in later periods of Christian history, let me introduce some additional categories into our discussion. As indicated earlier, we have recently gained access to important new research into the nature of *cura animarum* in the history of man's religions. Some of this research pertains to Christianity. A highly suggestive contribution is that of William Clebsch and Charles Jaekle in their book entitled *Pastoral Care in Historical Perspective.* They suggest that pastoral care in the history of the Christian churches has taken a variety of forms. All these forms are present at all times, but because of changing social circumstances the Christian churches had tended to emphasize some forms more than others at various times in history.

The four forms of pastoral care they mention have a deceptive simplicity about them. These are healing, guiding, sustaining, and reconciling. The first three of these were suggested to Clebsch and Jaekle from a typology developed by Seward Hiltner in his *Preface to Pastoral Theology.* The definitions assigned to these functions by these authors will help our discussion.

Healing is that function in which a representative Christian person helps a debilitated person to be restored to a condition of wholeness, on the assumption that this restoration achieves also a new level of spiritual insight and welfare.

Sustaining consists of helping a hurting person to endure and to transcend a circumstance in which restoration to his former condition is remote or impossible.

Guiding consists of assisting perplexed persons make confident choices when such choices are viewed as affecting the present or future state of the soul.

There are two forms of guidance.

Eductive guidance tends to draw out of the individual's own experiences and values the criteria and resources for such decisions. Inductive guidance tends to lead the individual to adopt an *a priori* set of values and criteria by which to make his decisions.

Reconciling functions to reestablish broken relationships between man and fellow man and between man and God.[1]

Let us now sample Clebsch and Jaekle's review of the history of Christianity and their understanding of which of these functions tended to be dominant in different periods. Clebsch and Jaekle assure us that in each period of Christian history which they discuss, all of the four functions of pastoral care were present. However, in each period, one function tended to be dominant because of the historical needs of the church in that period of time.[2] During the period of primitive Christianity, which lasted until around A.D. 186, pastoral care was characterized by an emphasis on sustaining souls through the vicissitudes of life in this world which Christians believed to be running swiftly toward its end. For the next hundred years, the pace of persecution of Christians by civil authorities accelerated. Many of these Christians, under the pressure of persecution, fell away or "lapsed" from the life of the church. During this period, the reconciliation of lapsed souls back into the life of the church became the central focus of the cure of souls. An important shift in the nature of pastoral care occurred after the establishment of Christianity as the official religion by the Emperor Constantine. Pastoral care then became a tool for assimilating various groups, especially the Teutonic people of the north, into the ethos of the empire and the church. During this period, pastoral care took on an increasingly inductive character. Clebsch and Jaekle believe that healing became important for the cure of souls during medieval times, reconciliation during the Renaissance and Reformation, sustaining during the Enlightenment, and finally an increasingly more eductive style of care during the late nineteenth century and the early twentieth century.

In the following discussion, I will not be bound by their organizational scheme. I mention their point of view primarily to suggest that a periodization is possible. The outline I will offer is not exhaustive. It is designed rather to advance the major interpretations that I wish to propose.

First, I am not certain that the categories of sustaining, guiding, and reconciliation are distinct. They may in fact be different phases or different moments in the general task of discipline. By discipline, I mean not just what occurs after someone has done something wrong. As I am using the term, discipline is certainly more than simply punishment or penance, although it may include these dimensions. Discipline is first of all a matter of deeply implanting within the character of a people the basic norms, patterns, values, and sensibilities that govern the culture of the group. Discipline, as the task of forming and maintaining the emotional sensibilities, values, and behavioral norms of a people called Christians, was very much the central task of pastoral care —in the early church, during the Dark Ages, and in the medieval church.[3]

The mode of discipline that predominated was influenced by changing circumstances. In turn, these changing circumstances influenced the shape of the expectation about time that governed the life of the Christian community. Care, discipline, and the structure of time—these are the coordinates from which I would like to view certain features of the history of the cure of souls in the Western world.

THE EARLY CHURCH

Sustaining Christians in the life of perfection until the final return of Christ was the modality of discipline in the first century of the Christian era. The time perspective was future-oriented, aiming toward an imminent but unpredictable end of this world and the beginning of a radically new world which Christians gradually began to view in increasingly more other-worldly terms.[4] The forgiveness of sins granted at baptism was to wipe away all former sins and inaugurate a life of perfection. The basic structure of the Jewish law and the Ten Commandments, radicalized by an ethos of Jesus' supralegalism but devoid of the restrictions of Jewish cultic law, provided much of the content of this image of perfection.[5] The life of perfection, seen as something of a holding operation until the Second Coming, was the basic goal of care as discipline and sustaining. Persons were advised to continue to support themselves,[6] the unmarried were not to marry (unless they could not control themselves otherwise),[7] and widows were to remain single.[8] Mutual edification *(aedificatio mutua)* and fraternal correction *(correptio fraterna)* were the primary styles of care as is generally the case in movements with little formal hierarchy.[9]

RECONCILING DURING THE PERSECUTIONS

The modality of discipline by sustaining was soon supplemented by another modality—that of discipline by reconciling. The occasion which brought forth this new mode of care was the rise of the persecutions against the Christian community. Although there had been persecutions during the entire Christian period, the major persecutions of Decius in the third century necessitated new mechanisms of discipline and reconciliation.[10] Could a person be reinstated in the Christian community after lapsing? What lapses, which sins, and what kind of backsliding could be forgiven? These were the primary issues during this period. Bishops arose to handle questions pertaining to reconciliation of the lapsed. Sins were codified systematically. The types of penance necessary for reinstatement were specified. The practice of *metanoia* (repentance) and *exomologesis* (public confession) became normative.[11]

The time perspective that dominated the consciousness of Christians began to shift. Anticipation about the imminent coming of Christ began to wane. In the face of this failure, the kingdom was seen now as a kingdom of heaven—a reward that the faithful Christian would receive at death. The individualistic elements of the New Testament story were accentuated. Once individual decision about the sayings of Jesus had been the key to whether a person would participate or not in the inevitable coming of the kingdom. Now individual good deeds, belief in the person of Jesus as the Christ, plus the baptismal blessings of the church determined whether a person would inherit the kingdom of heaven after death. Pastoral care was sustaining the faithful and reconciling the lapsed for the inheritance of this future time after death.

THE CURE OF SOULS IN THE IMPERIAL CHURCH

The next period marks a decisive shift in the mentality of the Christian religion with a concomitant shift in the nature of the cure of souls. In the fourth century, with the Constantinian establishment of the Christian church as the official church of the Roman Empire, Christianity loses the last vestiges of a pariah mentality—the mentality of a people on the outside, or a people harassed and oppressed by other more powerful and more established groups. Christianity was now the ingroup; others were the outgroups. The church, its bishops, and pastoral care were now cast into a new role, different from anything ever experienced before in Judeo-Christian history. The ancient symbols of a pariah people were reworked and utilized by an established church and empire for the purposes of controlling and assimilating the diverse groups, cultures, and nations of southern and northern Europe.[12]

This new task was assisted by the various brands of Platonic

62   *The Moral Context of Pastoral Care*

and Neoplatonic philosophy which saw the universe as a great hierarchical chain of being.[13] With the help of Plotinus and Augustine of Hippo, a model of the universe developed which saw the church, through its bishops and priests, as the controller of the traffic up and down this great chain.[14] The church was the keeper of the keys. The cure of souls was seen as various forms of guidance by which a person was inducted into progressively higher degrees of perfection along the chain of being.[15]

The Benedictine monks of the sixth century and their twelve-step ladder of humility provided a hierarchical model of pastoral care and discipline that gradually gained in popularity and influence.[16] The first three rungs of the ladder—to fear God, to despise one's own desires, and to obey the church—were thought appropriate for the layman as well as the priest and monk. In addition, during this period various penitential manuals were written which codified sins and specified appropriate penances.

The prominence of inductive guidance and the role of the church as an integrator of culture during the later Dark Ages and the medieval period has certain similarities with the role of Hinduism in the history of India.[17] Hinduism was the religion of the established, conquering princes and kings of the early Aryan civilization which came from the north, gradually assimilating the various tribes and groups of India.[18] These tribes and sibs—largely guest or pariah groups—became the basis of an early caste system. This caste system both incorporated yet kept duly segregated the newly acquired groups from the other more established classes. The doctrines of karma (the causal consequences of action) and samsara (the wheel of rebirth) helped articulate hierarchical order upon which a person could progress from life to life and rebirth to rebirth.

In the West, however, the hierarchical model was without the doctrine of reincarnation and without a system of castes. Partially because of the individualism of primitive Christianity, a person could progress up the ladder of spiritual purity to higher levels as an individual—possibly within a single lifetime. But in spite of these differences, ancient Hinduism and medieval Christianity performed a similar role in culture. Their respective methods of directing souls had some important resemblances as well. Both served as integrators of a diverse culture, assimilating human beings from the outside to the inside or from the bottom of the spiritual ladder to higher stations.

THE CURE OF SOULS
DURING AND AFTER THE REFORMATION

What happened at the level of the cure of souls during and after the Reformation is one of the most important chapters in the history of man's religion. Any time that you begin to depreciate the importance of pastoral care, remind yourself that it was over questions of conscience and guilt and how these are to be handled by the church that the Reformation began and one of the most dynamic periods of world history started to unfold. From the standpoint of our concerns, the Reformation marks the beginning of the instability that has marked the modern church—an instability between its theology and its specific modes of ordering and guiding everyday behavior and attitudes.

In the medieval Catholic Church, its theology of grace and forgiveness and its method for guiding everyday behavior were integrally related to produce a powerful method of inductive guidance. The bedrock of medieval Catholic theology, especially as it was influenced by Anselm and set forth in his famous *Cur Deus Homo,* was the belief that it was necessary to compensate God for sin. Since man owed perfect obedience to God to begin with, it was impossible to make up through penance for the gravity of even a single sin. One cannot pay back more than everything, and, according to Anselm, one owes everything to God (perfect obedience) to begin with. In order for a person to be saved, God arranged the perfect penance. The perfect penance was the sacrificial death of Jesus Christ (himself innocent from sin). This act was such a valuable repayment and compensation to God that it deposited enough merit to cover all the sins of mankind.[19] The parallel emphasis on penance in the theology of the eucharist and the everyday guidance of individuals was remarkable. The penitential manuals so widely used by the average priest during this period emphasized the necessity of the sinner compensating, through appropriate penances, for his sins. The sinner was to go as far with this compensation as possible; the grace which had accrued from Christ's sacrifice would make up the difference. The administration of grace through the sacraments helped relieve some of the excessive demands, but it did not disrupt the basically inductive method of guidance of the medieval Catholic Church. As James Barclay has said, it was "one thousand years of Christian behavioral modification."[20] This suggests that B. F. Skinner would know what was going on during this period. From the standpoint of behavioral scientists, Christianity during this time would be seen as primarily a religion of control.

The Reformation dealt a serious blow to the Catholic synthesis of theology and practical guidance. In addition, it saw a notable decline of several important aspects previously associated with the Judeo-Christian tradition of the cure of souls. What was lost was most of the ways in which this tradition had regularized methods for influencing and guiding the specifics of everyday life in its various spheres, such as family, economy, and politics. Gone in Luther's church were the penitentials with their calculus of sins and penances.[21] Gone was regular private confession (the public confession had been absent for centuries); informal and occasional private confession took its place.[22] Gone were the scribe and the rabbi of the Jewish faith who taught the Torah and Talmud through rational exposition. Gone, at least temporarily, were mutual edification and fraternal correction that characterized the practices of the early church. In their place were the doctrines of the priesthood of all believers, the radical sinfulness of man's will, the impossibility of salvation by works, and the most emphatic statement ever of salvation by God's immutable and sovereign grace.

Benjamin Nelson has proffered the thesis that the decline of the medieval system of the cure of souls is only partially explained by the general debasement it suffered. Its decline is also to be explained by certain turns in the development of Neoplatonic "illuminism" in the work of Bonaventura and Meister Eckhart. Their emphasis on the soul's rebirth, as a result of a mystical union with God, tended to undercut the direction of the soul by priest and penitential. In addition, medieval illuminism, it is commonly agreed, provided some inspiration for Luther's own theology, especially his concept of conscience.[23]

On the face of it, Lutheran innovations in the care of souls could have left the church with little or no influence over the day-to-day lives of people. In reality, it opened up a broader range of secular controls which the church itself indirectly both promoted and sanctioned. To understand this we must discuss once again the rise of the so-called Protestant ethic, the crucial importance of the Lutheran concept of vocation, the Calvinistic concept of predestination, and something about the new capitalist ethos that was emerging during the Renaissance.

The Lutheran doctrine of vocation had more influence on modern patterns of guidance than any other idea in Luther's thought. According to Luther, Christians could not earn their salvation, but it was their duty to respond to the free grace and forgiveness of God through service in their everyday lives. This service did not earn their salvation, but it was the way to express their gratitude for it. However, in the field of their secular vocations, they were to be subject to the secular and civil authorities who governed their particular roles in their vocation.[24] As Weber pointed out, this left Lutheran Christians with a sense that it was their God-ordained task to be faithful and obedient to the authorities of the secular and civil realm. It also *implicitly* suggested that they were to be obedient to whatever new patterns of economic activity were emerging in these realms. It is important to assert that Weber never said that Protestantism created capitalism; certainly, various unsophisticated forms had been developing during the Middle Ages.[25] But clearly, the Lutheran doctrine of vocation may have given rise to a certain type of personality —ready, conscientious, and malleable to the requirements of this new order.

But the Lutheran doctrine of vocation could not have been

enough to give rise to the so-called Protestant ethic and Protestant personality type. Modern capitalism took on a more elaborate process of rationalization than earlier forms of capitalism had ever done. Long-term planning for the future and complicated methods of accounting for credits and debits were part of this newer, more methodical capitalism. Obviously, the Lutheran doctrine of *Beruf* (vocation) did not account for this particular dimension of the spirit of capitalism. Something more was needed. Weber believed that the Calvinistic doctrine of predestination was the element that explained the rise of this additional component of character.[26] That doctrine affirmed that God in his sovereignty elected some men to salvation and others to damnation; no man could earn his salvation and no man could know he had actually achieved it. However, there arose in this situation a form of pastoral advice which said that worldly success and intense activity in the secular world were indeed signs that one had been elected.[27]

Weber believed that the time perspective implicit in the Calvinistic doctrine of predestination was important for developing among Reformed Christians a type of worldly asceticism of unusual dimensions. If the sign of one's election to everlasting heavenly reward was a lifetime of energetic activity marked with some worldly success, then it followed that one should indeed attempt to organize one's life in this way in order to convince oneself of one's election. Organizing one's life into a long series of delayed gratifications in an effort to generate material gain, but with no thought of actually enjoying this gain, gave rise to the rational-ascetic entrepreneur who became the Protestant personality type par excellence. According to Weber, Benjamin Franklin was the American patron saint of this type and *Poor Richard's Almanack* was the sacred text.[28]

If Weber was right, then we have in Reformed Christianity a new synthesis of churchly and worldly sources of guidance. In short, the church may have unwittingly guided men to be guided in turn by the needs of the emerging capitalist system.

Weber saw this synthesis operating in the concrete pastoral

care and guidance of the Reformed churches of Presbyterianism and Congregationalism. He also saw it, to some extent, among certain pietist groups, among the Methodists, and among the Baptists. To some extent, I believe, other researchers have confirmed the picture that he painted. Liston Mills, in his 1965 article entitled "The Relationship of Discipline to Pastoral Care in the Frontier Churches, 1800–1850 . . . ," shows that there was a remarkable similarity between the pastoral care practices of Presbyterian, Methodist, and Baptist churches on the American frontier.[29] They all tended to exert pastoral guidance through group meetings of one kind or another. The aim of these meetings was to protect and guide the Christian through the hazards of a sinful world in an effort to gain the rewards of eternal life. The Methodist band meetings were the most advanced form of this kind of care. These groups, and others as well, emphasized a method of mutual examination and fraternal correction as they tested each other's daily life and the state of the soul.[30] Once again, Methodism made explicit what was still latent in many groups during this period—an emphasis on a methodical organization of an ascetic life designed to show forth the signs of a saved soul. An ethics of economic life in the secular world was a persistent dimension of much of the pastoral care during this period. There can be little doubt that many of these people developed dependable and systematic orientations to their business affairs which indeed made them the most respected shop owners, bankers, clerks, and farmers in their communities.

It is interesting to note how important mutual edification and fraternal correction became in some Protestant churches. It is indeed reminiscent of the styles of group care and correction typical of the early Christian church. It is as though when guidance by settled centers of authority declines, guidance by the group must take its place. When the law and its interpretation by the rabbi declined in the early Christian community, direction by the group emerged. When the Catholic penitentials and confessional declined, fraternal correction arose to take its place. This was especially true of more pietistic groups in Lutheranism which developed around Bucer in Strasbourg or Spener in Frankfurt.[31] But it was equally true of certain Presbyterian, Methodist, and Baptist groups as well.

PASTORAL CARE IN THE MODERN PERIOD

This long presentation on the cure of souls is an effort to put the modern period more into perspective. Pastoral care in twentieth-century mainline Protestant churches has been vastly different from anything seen before in Jewish and Christian history. In general, we see a retreat from a structured and well-articulated religiocultural context for the practice of pastoral care. Pastoral care becomes one of two things. It becomes a process of pastoral visitation designed to oil the wheels of parish and church life in an increasingly pluralistic and mobile society,[32] or it becomes a short-term and rather faltering attempt to give consolation and encouragement to certain people with personal and private difficulties.[33] Books and articles discussing pastoral care as moral upbuilding of the members of the Christian church decline almost to the vanishing point. Although I do not want to suggest that maintaining the institutional church is unimportant, I want to concentrate on the emphasis on personal counseling. This is the type of care which has been most influenced by the dialogue between modern Protestant pastoral care and the so-called modern secular psychotherapies.

Much of modern pastoral care has been eductive. As I indicated earlier, in this it has adapted to several aspects of the cultural and social context of Western society in the twentieth century. These aspects have to do with the pluralism, rapid social change, and social differentiation of modern societies. In a pluralistic and rapidly changing society, all centers of authority, be they constructive or destructive, tend to lose their influence. Systems of values are no longer widely shared by the different groups within a society. This is true even of the church and its members. In modern pluralistic and rapidly changing societies, the church has far more difficulty being the exclusive or even predominant value influence on the lives of its people. It is quite understandable that in such a social context, pastoral care has tended primarily to become eductive counseling. Often, the minister was able to do no more than help troubled persons clarify their *own* value systems and use them as best they could to solve their own difficulties. It was at this point that pastoral care borrowed so freely from the insights and techniques of secular theories of counseling and psychotherapy, especially Rogerian client-centered counseling.[34] The social situation may have been just as important in influencing many pastors to adopt the methods of the newer therapies as was the alleged value or validity of the therapies themselves.

Yet this trend may have gone too far. It may be that an overemphasis on eductive guidance in an effort to function within the value assumptions of the troubled person has forgotten that the person's value framework may be in disarray. In addition, eductive counseling may fail to take seriously the nature of the Judeo-Christian tradition, a tradition which has attempted to form firm collectivities of people (the synagogue and the church) with the capacity for ethical action.

Let me conclude with a partial correction of Weber's Protestant ethic hypothesis. In doing this, I must refer to the thoughtful work of James Luther Adams.[35]

Weber was primarily an economist. He was chiefly interested in the relationship of Protestantism to economic behavior. For this reason, however, he may have been oblivious to the influence of Reformed Protestantism on political life—especially associational life in England and the United States. Partially on the basis of the group life within Reformed Protestant movements (the practices of mutual edification and fraternal correction), and partially on the basis of what Adams calls the "totalistic impulse" of Calvinism, certain quarters of Reformed Christianity had a peculiar genius for forming among themselves and with others all sorts of voluntary groups for the betterment of the whole society. Adams points out that Weber failed to "take into account the Calvinist view that the church and its members have the obligation to work for the establishment of a society of justice and mercy."[36] For Calvinists of the period, the Christian bears a general vocation in the world as well as having a specific calling in his daily work. Adams refers to this outlook as "the totalistic impulse" of the Calvinists, and a recognition of it has given rise to a new phase of the controversy over Weber's thesis.

The force of this comment is to suggest that ascetic inner-worldly Protestantism may have an impulse within it besides that which has made it such a worthy promoter and steward of rational capitalism and the quest for success. Protestant asceticism has a more fundamental thrust toward action designed to shape a more just and equitable society. Adams calls our attention to a remark of Ernst Troeltsch, who once wrote that Calvinists were given "to an organized and aggressive effort to form associations, to a systematic endeavor to mold the life of society as a whole, to a kind of Christian Socialism."[37] In addition, David Little has suggested that Puritans in England may have used their understanding of "covenant law" and applied this by analogy to the ordering of the larger society.[38] Calvinism was feeding on the oldest substrata of Jewish-Christian symbolisms because of the privileged place it gave to the Old Testament. That there is a drive toward systematic and responsible this-worldly activity in Reformed Protestantism need not be denied. But, as Winthrop Hudson has pointed out, it was probably not until the close of the seventeenth century that this emphasis on responsible action to bring about the just society degenerated to a narrower preoccupation with profit in the economic realm.[39]

Inner-worldly asceticism can be utilized to rehabilitate both the public and pastoral care ministry of the church. But once again, this can occur only when certain distortions in its orientation to life have been removed. Inner-worldly asceticism is usable only when this tradition is reinterpreted in the light of a philosophical anthropology. The need to give philosophical articulation to and philosophical confirmation of the anthropology of inner-worldly asceticism will be a topic of discussion later.

IV

Culture, Religion, and Care

Culture must be given an important place in any discussion of the context of pastoral care. I have the suspicion that most of today's helping disciplines are oblivious to the fact that care (psychotherapy, counseling, guidance) goes on in a cultural context of some kind. When a practitioner is oblivious to this fact, there is likely to be an exaggeration of the technical and scientific aspects of care and a blindness to the cultural assumptions, symbols, and goals that define the actual horizons of care. There is a tendency to see care as a set of specific acts that one does for another person, or as a set of scientific truths that are applied, or even as a matter of simple "love" or "concern" or "feeling" for another. This simple view fails to realize that whatever care is, it must take a point of departure from a culture and feed back into that culture, or seek to create an alternative culture. The recognition of this fact somehow escapes many practitioners in the helping disciplines, be they religious or secular in orientation.

Much of our discussion has not been about culture as a whole. It has dealt more specifically with the higher value assumptions of a culture, that level which I have often referred to as the religiocultural dimension. The religious dimension of a culture refers to the controlling values and value symbols that seem to shape the identity of a community (and many of the individual identities within the community) and organize lesser values pertaining to everyday actions, decisions, and procedures. The religiocultural value symbols of a people provide models for how a community should orient itself to certain broad categories of life. Such categories include time, space, nature, human vulnerability, the possibilities of human action, and the nature of human destiny.

We have looked at the religiocultural value symbols of the Protestant ethic, its secularized counterpart called "instrumental activism," and certain major themes in the Judeo-Christian conglomerate. We have traced to some extent the way in which these religiocultural contexts may have influenced the cure of souls or counseling and guidance.

I now want to give attention to several things. First, I want to delineate more completely a concept of culture and try to specify some of the various ways in which culture can be related to care, counseling, and guidance. Second, I want to talk more concretely about the major stages of mainline Protestant pastoral care in the recent past. I want to demonstrate how the major theories of pastoral care in the Protestant churches have failed to emphasize the importance of the religiocultural context of pastoral care. Third, I want to set forth a philosophical anthropology from which we might begin to evaluate the human serviceability of various religiocultural visions.

THE MEANING OF CULTURE

The concept of culture has come in for considerable reflection in recent years. The relationship between religion and culture has been a subject of vigorous inquiry. Paul Tillich, Clifford Geertz, and Benjamin Nelson are three of the more prominent scholars who have given special attention to this issue.[1] What follows is indebted to all of these thinkers, but attempts to rely on none of them in detail. The view of culture below must stand or fall on its own merits.

What are some of the components of culture? The word "culture," as I am using it, does not just mean what is implied when we say that a person is a "man of culture"—someone showing evidence of wide learning in the fine arts, history, and philosophy.

I would define culture to mean a set of symbols, stories (myths), and norms for conduct that orient a society or group cognitively, affectively, and behaviorally to the world in which it lives. Cultures give coherence, regularity, and commonality to a people, group, or society. Groups and societies have cultures. A single individual is a member of that group or society and feels compatible with it by virtue of sharing in the identity of that culture. Following Tillich, we can also say that religion is closely related to culture. It can be considered as its "inner core"—the "substance" or "depth dimension," or the ultimately serious dimensions of culture.

Cultures are generally maintained and articulated by myths, theologies, or certain coordinating models. In primitive societies, myths (narratives that answer questions about origins and destinies) often give coherence and legitimation to cultural values and norms. In more advanced societies, myths often give way to theologies—efforts to give systematic and more or less rational articulation to the meaning of the myth. It may be that in modern societies, theologies give way to abstract models about the nature or function of things, people, and society. These models may serve the same function as myths and theologies. They give certain members of the society (for instance its intellectual elites) kinds of maps which orient them to their worlds, tell them what to trust, what to hope for, and how to get what they have come to believe is the good. It may also be that these rather abstract models (models of the machine, the body, evolutionary-biological models, cybernetic models) are used to reinterpret the symbols of past theologies and inherited myths. This is certainly what has happened in the contemporary school of process philosophy and theology. Here scholars use models from theoretical physics and evolutionary biology to integrate and interpret certain facts about the physical world. Then these combined biophysical models are used to reinterpret certain basic philosophical concepts about the nature of God found in inherited theologies. Finally, these reworked philosophical ideas about God are used to reinterpret ancient myths.

These myths, theologies, or models give people some kind of

orientation in the cognitive, affective, and behavioral spheres of life. They provide men with images of what is true and what is good. For our purposes, we are primarily interested in how cultures help us gain orientation to the good. In this context, I will characterize the good as both that which is valuable (desirable) and that which is procedurally right or normative in gaining the valuable.

A good culture has within it the power to do three things— *(a)* to develop or nourish, *(b)* to pattern, and *(c)* to limit. With regard to the cognitive sphere, it stimulates knowing, patterns and channels the processes of knowing, and gives some hints, more or less clear, about what are the limits of knowledge. In the areas of affects and motivations, culture stimulates or activates useful emotions, patterns their expression, and limits certain emotions by giving indices of what is appropriate to express in various circumstances. In the area of behavior, culture encourages certain actions, patterns actions, and limits actions. For instance, certain actions are not to be taken at all, others are appropriate for certain occasions and not for others, with certain people and not with others. Cultures give models and maps that guide people in these areas.

Cultures give orientation to institutions as well as individuals. In fact, individuals can work in institutions and play a role in them because their culture gives them directives and orientations to the goals and procedures of institutions and what their own actions should be in the context of these institutions.

Finally, cultures always have a religious dimension about them, but only in some cultures is the religious dimension explicit and so named. As I indicated above, the religious dimension of the culture is that which is most central to the value structure of the culture—most central to that which people take seriously, or, as Tillich said, take ultimately. Recently, Western intellectuals have referred to the most widely shared common values of a particular culture as its "civil religion." In the case of our own culture, the official religion—the religion of the various churches and synagogues—may or may not reinforce the civil religion of our culture. Generally, it has. But there are rare exceptions when certain church groups at various times come into tension with the dominant values of the society. One example of this may have been the early dissent expressed by certain Christians and Jews against the Vietnam war. When such dissent is expressed, the churches may be projecting alternative cultural visions. A religious body always projects a religiocultural vision of some kind, even though it may be in tension with the dominant religiocultural vision of the larger society.

PASTORAL CARE IN RECENT TIMES

I now want to make a short review of the major recent trends in pastoral care in the mainline Protestant churches. What follows is not a sociological survey. I will make this review by concentrating on selected prominent theoretical statements about what *should* be happening. I am confining myself to written texts about pastoral care that many ministers have read and probably tried to imitate. The main purpose of this review is to assess the extent to which the literature of pastoral care takes sufficient account of its various religiocultural contexts.

From the perspective of the long view of Christian history, pastoral care in recent times has been primarily eductive. By eductive, I mean that the role of pastoral care has been to enable persons to recover lost or impaired capacities for decision and initiative. This was certainly the fundamental thrust in the Rogerian era of pastoral counseling, and its spirit is still with us. By providing the troubled person with a strong and supportive relationship (a relationship of acceptance, unconditioned positive regard, and empathy), the counselee could relax enough to sort out "real feelings," regain a "sense of confidence," and make some decisions which would carry life forward. The works of Seward Hiltner, Thomas Oden, Daniel Day Williams, and others, including myself, have made contributions to this approach.

Like so much of modern counseling or psychotherapy, this approach assumed a religiocultural context, even relied on it, but

seldom made it explicit in the caring relationship. The dimensions
of culture which related to the cognitive, emotional, and behavioral patterning of life were assumed; they were not directly invoked.

To this extent, this period was consistent with the attitude of
Freud. Freud did not discuss morality or ethics as such in the
context of counseling relationships. He assumed that once persons were rid of their neurotic conflicts, they would somehow
know what was right. Freud paid little attention to the question
of psychosynthesis—how to put the psychological world of the
troubled person back together again, after analysis had occurred.
Freud, however, was a Jew. Distance has taught us the extent to
which he unconsciously assumed a Jewish mind-set when it came
to questions of personal and social ethics. Philip Rieff's *Freud:
The Mind of the Moralist*[2] and David Bakan's *Sigmund Freud
and the Jewish Mystical Tradition* have demonstrated in different
ways the significant Jewish context to Freud's thought. The social
theorist Benjamin Nelson has also pointed out how Freud could
fail to emphasize psychosynthesis, partially because of his own
unrecognized assumptions about the capacity of persons to know
the good—assumptions most likely formed by his own unconscious adherence to his Jewish religiocultural tradition. Nelson
writes that Freud "fancied that there were very few moral
predicaments in the world, and he thought that almost everyone
would know precisely where the moral obligation was," once a
person was cured of his transference neurosis.[3]

The literature of modern pastoral care has taken much the
same approach. But in some ways the modern pastoral counselor
has had more difficulty than Freud had. The pastoral counselor
and his client during the middle of the twentieth century had not
unconsciously internalized a sense of the lawful as had Freud the
Jew. Furthermore, life in the United States was far less settled
with regard to moral issues during the 1940's, 1950's, and 1960's
than in European Vienna around the turn of the century when
Freud did most of his work.

The move toward eductive counseling was brought about by

several pressures in modern life. The example and prestige of the secular therapies was one of the forces. Diversity, complexity, and specialization of modern societies was another. These sociological factors have had a great impact on standards of social conduct. We do not have to argue that modern man is more or less moral to make the point that there is moral pluralism in both public and private behavior, and certainly to a higher degree in advanced societies than was previously the case. This has brought pressure on all counselors to back away from being directive or taking a position on moral and ethical matters in the situation of pastoral counseling and care. Instead, they play the role of the supporter, accepter, and clarifier.

In view of this situation, the following observations should be made. Issues of motivation, or capacity for action, are indeed distinguishable (logically and practically) from issues of right conduct. The modern therapies have made a contribution in demonstrating this distinction. It is often good for the counselor to stay at the level of feelings, motivations, and capacities without raising issues of normative conduct. This new insight, however, has sometimes been expanded to suggest an image of the good counselor as one who did not make moral judgments at all, in or out of therapy. There is a great difference between temporarily suspending moral judgments because the context of judgment is assumed or quite clear, and refusing to exercise judgment even when the context is not clear or is quite confused. Increasingly, the nonjudgmental attitude of all therapy—including Protestant pastoral counseling—has tended to operate in a climate of confused moral understanding. The concepts of acceptance, or even forgiveness, may be quite meaningless if a context of moral order and judgment is absent or confused. As was said earlier, citing the thought of Victor Turner, acceptance, forgiveness, love or communitas are meaningless and formless concepts without a context of moral norms, judgments, and structures.

The second period in pastoral counseling can be marked by the appearance of Howard Clinebell's *Basic Types of Pastoral Counseling,* published in the mid-1960's. Here Clinebell offered a revised model of pastoral counseling and care. In addition to the eductive and uncovering methods, he recommended procedures that were more directive and active to build up a person's strengths and activate his ego. This model combined the more dynamically oriented counseling attitudes of the Freudian-Rogerian period with methods that brought the pastor back closer once again to the image of an advice giver and spiritual director.[4]

In reality, however, the model was still eductive. Not once in the book is there a discussion of the cultural and moral context assumed by these more directive approaches, and what this context might actually mean for personal and public conduct. In Clinebell's important book, the usefulness of more directive counseling is often tied to the client's need for "information," "facts," and "skills."[5] The troubled person at times will need to be told where to go for financial assistance, medical aid, or other kinds of practical assistance relevant to solving part or all of the problems. The call for more directive and ego-building counseling and care takes on a primarily technical overtone. It falls short of confronting the more basic problem of how the pastoral counselor relates to the moral and value issues that may be at stake in the person's problems.

On the other hand, because the book does approach the issue of "directive counseling" it can easily be misconstrued to suggest that in the intimacy of the counseling relationship the pastor should take positions readily on moral issues and convey this as *a* central, if not *the* central, part of the counseling process. This is not what Clinebell had in mind. Unless there is explicit clarification of how the counselor actually relates to ethical issues, the concept of directive counseling can easily be so misunderstood.

I take the position that it is precisely because the minister is working in the context of a church community which is always attempting to clarify its value commitments, that on many occasions the pastor indeed would have the privilege of temporarily bracketing moral issues in his care. This does not mean that moral issues are irrelevant to the counseling process, or that love and acceptance conquer all. Rather, it means that the minister can afford, by virtue of the clarity of his moral context, to bracket moral issues temporarily for the sake of concentrating more specifically on dynamic, motivational, and emotional issues.

In other words, because the troubled person has some sense for where the pastor stands on certain moral issues, the minister, by not pouncing immediately on the value issue at stake, can avoid contributing to the further disintegration of the value framework of the individual or the larger society. If the minister's value stance emerges out of a process of value inquiry that comes forth from the community he represents, he can come nearer to avoiding moralism by sharing with the troubled person the best results of that explicit inquiry. More about this later.

There is a further difficulty with the position worked out in Clinebell's book. We must ask, what guides the pastor's actions in these more directive theories when he tries to build on a person's strengths and stimulate a stronger ego? Clinebell's answer sounds plausible and Christian, but it may be incomplete. The counselor tries to increase the person's capacity to establish "mutually-need-satisfying relationships" and to show forth "love of God and neighbor."[6] Without, however, a more specific discussion of the nature of human need and the marks of love, we have in this position once again communitas without structure, love without law. Hence, we do not know whether love means giving another person a massage, sleeping with his wife, inviting him to a cocktail party, joining him for a potluck dinner, or what. We need to know the indices of love—the marks of love.

This then leads to the third major stage in the recent development of the theory of Protestant pastoral care. This employs the new methods of the T-group, growth group, sensitivity training, or encounter group as a vehicle for training persons in the art of koinonia, Christian fellowship, and love. This is probably the most powerful emerging model. It uses the processes of group interaction to reveal to the participants of the group the way other persons perceive their actions. An open atmosphere of mutual sharing and feedback is encouraged. Through this process, it is hoped that persons will come to know themselves better, learn to trust other people more, share with others more easily, and develop more satisfying ways of relating to these persons. They are expected to learn through feedback how their attitudes, feelings, and behaviors come across to the other members of the group. The similarities of these methods to certain forms of pastoral care found in the early church and in some branches of reformation Christianity has been observed by many, most notably by Thomas Oden in his *The Intensive Group Experience.*[7]

These methods represent the most extreme manifestation of the modern tendency to talk about pastoral care without specifying its religiocultural context. As Kurt Back has said in his sociological study of this movement in its secular context, the primary goal of these groups seems to be an amorphous experience of "warmth," with a special emphasis on "experience."[8] Evidently they fulfill a great need for many "love-starved" and lonely persons in our transient and anomic modern societies.[9] Yet these groups, under certain kinds of leadership, can have considerable power to confuse persons about the values and behavioral norms that give structure and form to their lives. The valuational and normative context of such groups is often *sub rosa,* open to manipulation by the leader, and frequently unstable. It is quite possible that when these groups function in the context of a local church or in the context of a specialized pastoral counseling center, they operate in no fundamentally different way than in an ostensibly secular situation. On the other hand, it is quite possible that they do function differently in these more ecclesiastically oriented contexts. It all depends on the leadership and what is done in regard to the religiocultural context.

A PHILOSOPHICAL MODEL OF MAN

I now want to set forth a philosophical anthropology and discuss some of its implications for religion and some of its possible implications for care in a religious context. It has been my contention that the visions of the human implicit in inherited religious myths and stories need to be submitted to a philosophical analysis and justification. This is necessary for a variety of reasons. One does not do this if one is content only to understand and interpret the myth as it stood in the context of its own time and place. But if the claim is made that this story or myth is relevant to us in the situation in which we find ourselves in the last half of the twentieth century, then some kind of critical assessment must be made of this claim. This is true even with regard to our inherited religious commitments. Unless we are to be blind servants of whatever tradition we have received, we must find a critical perspective with which to review and examine our faith. I put myself in that tradition of *fides quaerens intellectum* (faith seeking understanding) which traces back through Anselm to Augustine. This position is quite consistent with the way the discipline of sociology presently describes how our thinking is related to our social conditioning and learning. Reflection always begins in the context of learned religiocultural assumptions. It is impossible to begin the processes of rational testing *de novo* and to suspend completely our learned commitments. However, it is possible—I would contend—to think critically about our faiths and our assumptions. It is also my conviction that the human mind, through a process of rational and critical reflection, actually can break through its own presuppositions and assumptions and see something new that previously was impossible to detect.

The model of philosophical anthropology I want to present has crystallized around studies into the way various species of biological organisms creatively adapt to the changes and challenges of their environment. The model comes from advances over the last hundred years in evolutionary biology and related areas. For purposes of shorthand, one might refer to it as the model of "creatively adaptive populations." It is an interpretation of certain scientific theories about how populations survive and thrive. But in addition, what follows here moves beyond fact and abstract model. It takes on the features of metaphor and story.

The idea of creative adaptation, in the context of evolutionary theory, primarily has reference to communities or populations of organisms.[10] Specialists who study species from this perspective attempt to discover what various species do to maintain and enrich their lives in and through their responses to the challenges of their environment.

Certain models of adaptation begin to emerge from this study. First of all, the adaptation that a species develops between itself and its environment is achieved. The adaptation is always a result of a delicate interplay between organism and environment. The environment in some way influences, changes, and selects certain aspects of the organism of the species and, on the other hand, the organism changes, influences, and selects certain aspects of the environment. Successful adaptation generally contains within it two movements: (1) the movement whereby the organism adjusts itself to fit the environment and (2) the movement in which the environment in some way is shaped or mastered to fit the species.[11] Weber's grand typology of world religions is based partially on a similar distinction. His division between mysticism and asceticism is meant to communicate this distinction between adaptation through adjustment (or internal manipulation of the self) and adaptation through mastery (external organization of reality). Parsons writes:

> Both resignedness and mastery are strategies to maintain or enhance personal dignity within the frame of reference. The path of mastery Weber calls asceticism, that of resignedness—or "adjustment," if one wishes to use that term—he calls mysticism. Both paths are orientations to the human condition as a whole, available to societies as well as to individuals.[12]

Once we make this distinction, we must point out that adaptation seldom if ever relies on one or the other strategy of adaptation. It is clear, however, that in any given strategy of creative adaptation, either adjustment or mastery will predominate.

The avoidance of death, according to this model, is an important motivational factor in animal and human adaptation. Individuals and species do what they can to survive. But, from an evolutionary-biological perspective, the death of the species is far more important than the death of the individual. From an evolutionary perspective, adaptation is primarily a species phenomenon designed to avoid the extinction of the species.[13] The natural death of the individual is necessary in order to make room for the young and the revitalizing energies that they contribute.[14]

Patterns of adaptation are both inherited and learned and the balance between learned factors and inherited factors varies notably from species to species. The inherited factor is the genetic code and the various potentialities for action that can be selected out of this pool for adaptive purposes. The learned factor is the pool of learned responses which, although they build on and pattern genetic capacities, do not in themselves have the status of inborn genetic structures.[15] The learned dimension of adaptive responses is greater in some species than in others. This dimension, in whatever species, can be referred to as the "culture" of the species. The culture, which always builds on and amplifies raw biological capacity, further patterns this capacity to deal with certain fine points of the adaptive process that the genetic code itself is insufficient to handle. Cultural symbols, then, are absolutely essential control mechanisms (to use the jargon of the biologist and the cyberneticist). They amplify, pattern, and limit the genetic capacities and the developmental sequences of the biological organism. Geertz points to the importance of cultural symbols for human adaptation when he writes:

> Such symbols are thus not mere expressions, instrumentalities, or correlates of our biological, psychological, and social existence; they are prerequisites of it. Without men, no culture, certainly; but equally, and more significantly, without culture, no men.[16]

There is room within this model for a creative element. Many biologists and biologically oriented theorists believe there is evidence to indicate that not only do biological organisms strive to survive but they strive to enrich and complexify experience.[17] Those who read the evolutionary pilgrimage in this way are often called emergent evolutionists. Evolutionary adaptation has a general direction (but no specific goals), according to this point of view. This direction includes sheer survival, but goes beyond it to include complexification and enrichment of forms and experience.[18] Those believing this are not just the philosophers and theologians such as Bergson, Whitehead, and Teilhard de Chardin.[19] There are respected biological specialists who say much the same thing. Theodosius Dobzhansky and L. Charles Birch are two of the more prominent who could be named.[20]

Let me summarize certain implications which this evolutionary model suggests to me about the normative organization of human energies. The two movements of adaptation through mastery and through resignation constitute the basic rubrics that will guide my discussion. Several different theorists have used various terms for these two movements. Heinz Hartmann seems to echo these distinctions with his classification of human action into alloplastic and autoplastic adaptation, i.e., adaptation that aims at a change in the external world and adaptation that proceeds primarily through self-manipulation and self-alteration. A slightly different set of distinctions is David Bakan's concepts of agency and communion. Agency refers to a modality of adaptation through mastery, and communion refers to a strategy of adaptation through receptivity.[21] Years ago, Whitehead tried to convey much the same distinction with his division of perception into presentational immediacy (the active, structuring mode) and causal efficacy (the holistic, intuitive mode).[22] More recently, advances in psychoanalytic ego psychology and research in altered states of consciousness have added new perspectives on these distinctions. Arthur Deikman has used the terms "activity" and "receptivity" to refer to different levels of ego functioning—the first of which actively structures, limits, and categorizes experience into the relatively safe and efficient everyday world that we need for biological survival and the second of which is more holistic, spatial, and intuitive.[23] This bimodal model of consciousness resonates with recent research—summarized in Robert Ornstein's *The Psychology of Consciousness*—into the functions of the two hemispheres of the brain, the left dedicated to analysis and linear thinking and the right specialized in more holistic, intuitive, and relational modes of thinking.[24]

Research into altered states of consciousness over the last ten years suggests that what often appears to be a resigned and passive dimension of many mystical states is actually a process of destructuring and temporarily setting aside the dominant rational and linear thinking typical of normal everyday activity (activity under the control of the left hemisphere of the brain). Various methods of mystical technique are designed to "deautomatize" or "destructure" this dominant modality of consciousness so that the more intuitive, holistic, and unitive modes of consciousness under the control of the right hemisphere of the brain can come to the fore.[25]

It is clear that creative adaptation to the challenges of any ecological niche necessitates utilization of both movements. The movement of mastery is of crucial importance for the human animal. Why is this the case? It is simply because human beings have a rich, flexible, and plastic set of instinctual equipment which does not guide them into an automatic adjustment with the environment. Man must create a world in which to live; he cannot simply conform to a natural world as it is. He must order a world; he must create a culture. The necessity to create a world to live in points to the fundamental importance of the adaptive movement through ascetic mastery.

But the movement through mastery alone is not only impossible, but finally destructive. Through this mode alone, man can construct a world that may become too impervious and blind to the realities of the larger environment in which he lives. Man then needs to break out of this constructed world into some kind of larger vision. This is where the more resigned and receptive mode becomes of crucial importance. It helps us to break—at least temporarily—out of our constructed worlds of meaning. This sometimes leads to the gaining of a larger vision; or sometimes it leads to a relaxation of the tenacity with which a person or community adheres to the constructed worlds that they in fact have.

I suggest that in Christianity we have a unique combination of

the two modes of consciousness. Ancient Judaism and its emphasis on practical rationality, the ordering of everyday activity
through the appeal to the covenant law, clearly endowed with a
certain sacredness a unique style of inner-worldly ascetic mastery.
Early Christianity, with its emphasis on the in-breaking of the
kingdom of God, the experience of Christ's spiritual presence,
and the possibility of forgiveness in the present moment, certainly
shifted the sense of the sacred toward a unique organization of
a more resigned yet unifying and holistic mode of consciousness.
It has been my argument that early Christianity with its emphasis
on these more unifying, holistic, and receptive modes of consciousness always must be understood in its Jewish context. The
Christian emphasis on the in-breaking of the spiritual presence
must be understood in the context of the Jewish emphasis on
practical moral rationality. Once this is understood, we can see
in primitive Christianity a unique fund of symbols and adaptive
strategies. These give the community fed by this tradition the
capacity to shift its sense of the sacred back and forth between
practical moral rationality (ascetic mastery) and the more resigned yet unitary modes of consciousness so necessary for the
destructuring and creative renewal of our everyday moral-
rational ordering of the world.

We have returned again to the distinction between structure
and communitas. In using the language of the left and right
hemispheres of the brain, I do not mean to suggest that the Jewish
use of the Torah or the Christian emphasis on the spiritual presence can be reduced to a contrast between physiological mechanisms. Clearly, the unique religiocultural meanings of these two
traditions cannot be exhausted by such a terse characterization.
Yet this characterization is useful if it is not allowed to consume
the hermeneutical task that is required to understand these traditions. This rather gross reductionism—and I am acknowledging
it as such—if not allowed to be the entire story, can give us a
"diagnostic indicator" (to use a phrase of Paul Ricoeur's)[26] of the
adaptive significance of the conglomeration of symbols synthe-
sized in early Christianity. The Christian community should be

precisely the community that will attempt to order the world into a just society through practical ethical principles and yet live out of a sense of participating in the life-giving spirit of God. This sense of God's presence will support the Christian amid his moral deliberations, his moral failures, and his need to be forgiven and renewed to pursue again the just ordering of life.

The mode of consciousness that we have called the receptive mode provides us with our sense of mystical union with the world. The time orientation in the receptive mode is the present, the moment, the existential now. This unitive experience in the present tense was symbolized in the Gospel narratives by the present in-breaking of the kingdom of God and later by Christ's spiritual presence within the Christian community.

But it is within the context of a long history of the Jewish emphasis on the active mode of practical moral rationality that this new emphasis on the receptive mode occurs. The active mode is still operative. There are signs of the kingdom of God in the present, but its full realization is to come in the future. This orientation toward the future is a sign that the active consciousness of Judaism still survives in primitive Christianity. Arthur Deikman writes, "In the time dimension, the action mode is the Future and the receptive mode is the Now." The continued presence of symbols of hope and renewal in the future demonstrates the contextual significance to primitive Christianity of the active mode so typical of Judaism.

The adaptive significance of the receptive mode can be seen in its capacity to get us in touch with the unitary and relational aspects of reality. It gives us a vision of our relatedness to the world, to other human beings, and to God. To this extent, the receptive mode is responsible for our visions of peace and wholeness which mark the religious sensibility. In the case of primitive Christianity, this vision, partially experienced in the present, is projected on the future. In this way, the receptive mode makes an essential contribution to the active mode—in this case the typically Jewish mode of practical moral rationality. To believe that this mode of practical moral rationality was dead in early

Christianity is to overlook the heavy traces of practical moral seriousness in such central witnesses as the Gospel of Matthew and the letters of Paul, especially to the Corinthians and the Thessalonians.

EVOLUTIONARY THEORY, RELIGION, AND CARE

The use of evolutionary theory to account for certain facts and forms of religion has a long history.[27] Frequently it has been misused. Nevertheless this model of explanation is still with us and has received some rather powerful restatements in recent years. In the following remarks, I will be drawing from the writings of Eugene d'Aquile, Charles Laughlin, Clifford Geertz, and Anthony Wallace.

I have argued that religion is closely related to culture. In primitive societies, it can be said that they often are identical. Religions, at least in part, are a result of man's efforts to develop a set of symbols, stories, and rituals that solve dichotomies and establish the basic adaptive strategy guiding a particular people.[28] Religion is the way in which a system of cultural control and organization is legitimated and given the appearance of durability and consolidation.

Let us be reminded of what we said earlier about the function of cultures. We said that some animals rely more on culture or learned behaviors than do other animals. It is often said that man is the animal par excellence of culture. This is true because of man's richly varied yet unstable biological equipment. Man's genetic code is highly important for his adaptation, but it is also clear that man's myriad instinctual capacities operate with far less precision, mechanical regularity, and specificity of purpose than is the case with animals lower on the evolutionary scale. Therefore, man's biological adaptation must be supplemented with culture. Culture is the pattern of symbols, values, and behavioral norms that guide and give appropriate expression to, yet also restrain, man's rich but plastic biological equipment.

Religion, especially in more primitive societies, seems to be the legitimating and sanctioning dimension of the cultural system that a particular people have hit upon to guide adaptation. The essence of the culture is often found in the symbols, stories, and myths that the society devises to convey its understanding of itself, its origins and destiny. Even more specifically, the basic story of a people will often contain within it a synthesis of some felt or experienced conflict which the society has at some time confronted.[29] Myths and sacred stories have a close relationship with cult life and ritual. Some scholars—Anthony Wallace is one of them—believe that myth tends to grow out of ritual.[30] Ritual tends to reenact an essential pattern of daily activity on which cultural cohesion depends. Ritual detaches this essential pattern from the concreteness of everyday life and enacts it symbolically. In the playful, symbolical reenactment of the pattern, the people gain inspiration and clarification and return to everyday life with a firmer sense of the central values in which they will place their trust.

How would we specify the nature of the care of souls (pastoral care, therapy, counseling, guidance) in the context of this evolutionary-biological interpretation of the nature of religion? Religion as a method to gain adaptation, organization, and control for a society will probably be serviced by officiaries, be they shamans, priests, or pastors. In primitive societies, these officiaries will enact certain rituals or intervene in informal ways to help groups and individuals who in some way fail to manifest the normative behaviors exemplified by the myth and ritual of the society. Failure to conform to the cultus may be due to an individual's own voluntary act or to some cause beyond the individual's control. In the first instance, his deviance might be called sin or crime; in the second, it might be called sickness—although in primitive societies these distinctions were seldom made with clarity. For either reason, the officiary or his lay representatives try to devise methods to incorporate the deviant individual back into the major strategy of adaptation developed by the community and upheld by the religion.[31]

All this becomes much more complicated in advanced societies because they have achieved a high degree of structural differentiation. By structural differentiation I mean that the various secondary institutions of a society begin to develop a relative autonomy from one another and from the central cultural organizing institution which deals with religion. In order to fulfill their proper cultural role in such societies, religions always should be both creating *and* maintaining the moral universe of those societies. Religion should both create and maintain, and sometimes in fairly rapid succession. It should make, modify, and remake a moral world. To be able to do so, religion in complex societies must have a floating sense of the sacred and necessarily move back and forth between structure and communitas. Care, in such societies, must always include the incorporation of persons into a given moral universe. But it must do more. Moral universes in advanced societies, and the stories and myths told to create and maintain them, are always in a process of change. Therefore, care at the highest level must consist primarily of "moral inquiry," employing various procedures for incorporating people into the process of creating workable syntheses of moral and religiocultural visions.

V

Toward a Model of Care

I want to outline a model for the embodiment of care. I will be saying a great deal about the church and the pastoral care of the church. In doing this, I do not want to suggest that the church is the only locus of care in our society. But I do contend that the functions of religion are crucial to the processes of care of a society. Therefore, what goes on in the church can be of great importance for the care exercised by the larger society. The church is one, but certainly not the only, source of religion in modern societies. When I speak of the church I have primarily in mind the mainline Protestant churches, although much of what I have to say could include large portions of Catholicism and Judaism as well.

The understanding of the church that I want to set forth draws heavily on the theology of my colleague James Gustafson.[1] However, I will expand his thinking in a variety of directions and add justifications for this view of the church, which will be largely my own. The view of the church that I present sees it as a center for moral discourse and decision-making. It sees the church as the historic bearer of an ethical sensibility that permeates the larger society. It sees the church as a place where the ethical capacities of the rest of society can be both stimulated and shaped.

Such a view assumes that the Judeo-Christian conglomerate is basically an ethical type of religion. It is a tradition which believes that ethical human action can meliorate the dichotomy between the actual and the ideal. This is true whether such action is seen as the condition for the coming of the kingdom (Judaism) or as the response to the in-breaking of this kingdom (Christianity).

The emphasis on moral discourse and moral decision-making is consistent with this view of the Judeo-Christian conglomerate. Religions of an ethical type are characterized by an emphasis on preaching and moral teaching. This is why they are religions of the "word" and of the "book." In simpler societies, ethical communities may have been formed primarily by highly gifted moral geniuses (Moses) or intellectual elites (priests). Such persons established moral visions and moral rules and passed them to the wider community by preaching, teaching, and recording these visions and rules in sacred texts. In the context of modern societies, however, to refer to the church as a community of moral *discourse* suggests a more inclusive process. The development of a moral ethos and sets of moral rules must necessarily involve dialogue between the individual members of the church and also between the church and its historical inheritance.

Another justification can be given for seeing the church as a community of moral discourse and decision. Not only is it consistent with the genius of the Judeo-Christian conglomerate, it is also consistent with the functions of religion in society as I set them forth earlier. There we observed that, at the societal level, religion performs a task of world construction. By this we mean that it projects the most controlling myths, stories, and value symbols by which a society lives. In the case of the Judeo-Christian tradition, there must be a certain type of world construction that goes on if it is to be true to its unique dimensions. The church as a bearer of this tradition must seek to build an ethical world —a religiocultural world which depicts the possibility of meaningful ethical action. Not all the worlds that religions build envision the possibility of meaningful action. In fact, if Arthur Danto can be believed in his recent *Mysticism and Morality,* the possibility of efficacious individual moral action is not provided for in the religiocultural worlds that most of the Eastern religions build.[2] Danto and Weber are in fundamental agreement on this point, whether or not they are correct in their judgments about Eastern religions. From my position, the world-building that the church should do is that which depicts the possibility of meaningful ethical action.

The task of religion is to construct a world. The task of the church is to construct an *ethical* world, a world in which forgiveness and renewal simultaneously are possibilities. But what would these two ideas mean in the context of modern societies of rapid social change? It means that the church, in an effort to perform both its general religious task and the task special to its own historical tradition, must create, maintain, modify, and re-create the value symbols of its ethical vision. The church must involve symbols themselves in a rhythm of creation, maintenance, and revision. This is the only way that a truly ethical religiocultural world can be successfully developed. If the church only maintains past moral worlds, it becomes authoritarian and no longer performs realistic and free ethical action designed to combat evil.[3] If it only creates, if it casts its lot with novelty and ceaseless revision, it is simply yielding to the pressures of the moment without testing the efficacy of its own time-proven moral visions and moral rules. It is clear that the church, in order to create and maintain a vision of an ethical religiocultural world, must alternate perpetually between its traditional priestly and prophetic roles if it is to perform its function in societies of rapid social change. This is true even if much of its function is to help reject large portions of the social change that various technological innovations make possible. Rapid social change under the pressure of technological innovation will continue in modern societies. Even if our society does a better job in the future than it has in the past of refusing certain possibilities that technology presents, still the cadence of change will exceed anything man ever knew before the twentieth century.

How can the church help construct a moral religiocultural world in a society of rapid social change? In attempting to answer this question, I will get to the heart of why I have chosen to refer to the church as a community of moral discourse and action. In a society where change is a pervasive characteristic, the church must assume that whatever revelation, insight, and wisdom it receives from the past, these can never be unambiguously applied to the novel situations that arise. Therefore, our moral visions and moral rules must be shaped through a process of inquiry. The moral visions and moral rules that have dominated the inherited tradition of the Judeo-Christian conglomerate are major resources informing the ethical discourse of the church. But they must be interpreted in open deliberation. And they are not the only resources that must be considered.

What I am saying is this: it is more important to be faithful to the general character of the Judeo-Christian religious tradition than it is to be faithful to the specific ethical rules which that tradition may have created to meet the needs of unique historical epochs. To characterize the church as a community of moral discourse and inquiry may be the best way to be faithful in our type of society to the inner genius of this tradition. Let me hasten to assure you that by characterizing the church as a community of moral discourse marked by a style of moral inquiry, I do not mean to say that the church should become nothing more than a debating society. I do not say that it should do away with worship, ritual, fellowship, and mutual care. Rather, the church should be characterized by all these dimensions. It is my specific task to demonstrate how they can all fit together and constitute the context of care.

THE HIERARCHY OF CARE

I want to set forth a hierarchical scheme for an understanding of the context of care. If the church is to exercise care for the present and the future, and if this care is to be manifest in specific acts of pastoral concern, then something like the following scheme of things may be necessary. I emphasize the hierarchical character of the model that I am about to present. By this I mean to suggest that the dimensions of the model which are presented first have a certain centrality about them. The higher levels of the hierarchy are important in and of themselves as crucial marks of the church; but in addition, they are determinative for the context and integrity of the dimensions lower in the hierarchy. Without the central elements of the model, the other dimensions can easily lose their character as functions of the church.

I am fully aware of the dangers of hierarchical thinking. What I have located at lower levels of the hierarchy are not unimportant and therefore to be neglected. But in an effort to restore some balance to our picture of the church as a whole, I take the risk of speaking hierarchically in a distinctively unhierarchical age.

Central to the life of the church—even its pastoral care—is the ministry of preaching. Whether preaching is done by the professional minister, by laymen, or by both, in order for the church to become a community of moral discourse, inquiry, and action, preaching must be central to its life. This is consistent with the Protestant emphasis on the centrality of the Word. But in the context of this model, preaching must be understood primarily as a matter of moral inquiry. And it should spring out of, reflect, and feed back into the ongoing moral inquiry of the total church. I will amplify.

Gone is the day when preaching can be understood primarily as a professional, ordained minister telling his more or less poorly informed congregation about the meaning of the Scriptural tradition and how it relates to the problems of everyday living. In a highly differentiated, pluralistic, and rapidly changing society marked by a wide distribution of highly specialized information, this model of preaching will not work. And if it appears to be working, one can only conclude that the church in question is something other than a community of moral discourse and action.

Nonetheless, preaching is of the utmost importance, but it should be understood as a method of summarizing, enriching, and further stimulating the ongoing moral inquiry of the worshiping community. Let us assume that we are speaking about the preaching of the professional ordained minister in a typical Protestant church. In order to do the kind of preaching I have in mind, the minister would have to establish one or two highly important subgroups in his congregation. These groups would be dedicated to an ongoing process of moral inquiry. In addition, they would have it as their task to feed the results of their inquiry back into the church and to help the church develop specifiable positions on a variety of moral issues. The actual mechanisms by which this would work will vary, depending on the polity of the particular church in question.

The role of the minister with regard to these groups would be to stimulate this moral inquiry. In fact, the major competence of the minister in this kind of church would be his training in moral reflection and moral inquiry. The preaching of the minister—as the chief stimulator and facilitator of these groups—would constitute, for the most part, a dialogue between himself and the concerns occupying the deliberations of these special moral inquiry groups. Hence, the authority of the minister in his preaching is a shared and multivalent authority. It would be an authority based on the Judeo-Christian tradition from which he spoke, the rules for moral reflection that he has learned, and the collective moral inquiry of his church and these special groups.

The topics that would occupy the inquiry of the congregation should reflect the major cultural and social dilemmas that beset Western society. This could range anywhere from the ethics of world food distribution to the ethics of sexuality. But since I have been addressing primarily the pastoral care of the church, let me list topics that are immediately relevant to this function. For the church to enact its pastoral care successfully, it must place its care in the context of a "practical theology" that addresses a variety of practical moral issues that are invariably fundamental to the context of care. To exercise pastoral care, the church must make progress on these practical moral issues. This is the task of its moral discourse.

What are some of these practical moral issues? Their number boggles the imagination. A plethora of social and cultural dilemmas face our rapidly changing society. I will mention only a few. Before the church can care for or counsel couples with disturbed marital relations, it must have some position on a practical theology of marriage and of male-female relationships. Before the church can care for or counsel people with sexual problems, it must have devised a practical theology that specifies the place of sexuality in the total scheme of a person's life. For the church to care for or counsel couples having difficulties raising their children, the church must have a theology of parent-child relationships. Before the church can care for or counsel the aging and the aged, it must have a fund of meanings that will enable its people and the larger society to understand the place of aging in life— it must have a practical theology of aging. To help persons who are ill, mentally or physically, the church must have a context of meaning in which to place the phenomenon of illness. Consider the issue of divorce. This is a problem that more and more will face the congregations of our society as the rate of divorce gradually climbs. Before the minister starts counseling a couple contemplating divorce, wouldn't it be well to deal with this within a context of meanings, more or less shared and assumed by the members of the church? When is divorce legitimate? What are the mutual obligations of the couple to examine themselves and their motives before the divorce? What fair and just procedure is to be followed in getting the divorce? I could go on and on.

The major difficulty with the pastoral care of the church today is that ministers are attempting to care for and counsel persons without the support of a fund of meanings that provide the context of understanding for the problems that the minister and the congregation are facing. This, by the way, is a major difficulty with all care and counseling in our society, religious and secular. The contexts of meanings, the normative value symbols governing the provinces of personal problems, are diffuse and vague. To take one example, our visions about what marriage should be are so vague that the counselor (religious or secular) often feels unable to assume anything normative. He must content himself with the more technical emotional-dynamic dimensions which do not interfere with the increasingly more pluralistic value commitments of people in our society on this issue. It should be the virtue of the church, and of the care and counseling which proceed under its auspices, that it would provide this context of normative meaning so increasingly difficult to achieve in our pluralistic and rapidly changing society. But the same forces that make it increasingly difficult for the secular counselor to assume a framework of normative meanings also strongly affect the capacity of the church to create and maintain a fund of normative meanings even for its members, not to mention the larger society.

But it is clear that the minister, even more than the secular counselor or therapist, has as a part of his responsibility to help create, maintain, and revise the normative value symbols of his society. This is the minister's first and foremost contribution to the exercise of care for troubled persons in our society, both the care that he and his congregation exercise and the care that secular counselors and institutions exercise. Without this more or less stable fund of normative meanings, neither he nor the secular counselor will have the luxury to bracket these meanings and concentrate primarily on dynamic and emotional issues. Without a fund of normative religiocultural meanings and symbols, the general confusion about the nature of the good in living will itself be enough to cause untold personal difficulties, muddled lives, overt illnesses and emotional conflicts.

It is being recognized increasingly that value conflicts and value ambivalences are themselves a major cause of problems in living and in even the more severe forms of mental illness.[4] One of the strongest assets to good mental health is the existence of a relatively firm and accurate moral universe which gives indices to the good and suggests appropriate actions to reach the good. Without this fund of normative meanings, it is impossible to make elementary distinctions between things that are good and things that are ill or criminal in character. Unless there are stable normative meanings pertaining to marriage, sexuality, aging, work, divorce, etc., there is no way for the counselor (religious or secular) to know if and when he is dealing with emotional incapacity and illness. As Parson suggests, the only way to define illness is with reference to the incapacity to fulfill the expectations connected with a normative order of meaning.[5] This truth is now beginning to be recognized even within the thinking of some secular counselors. They are finding it increasingly difficult to do counseling and psychotherapy with clients who are deeply confused about their own value commitments. What might look to the counselor like an issue of incapacity ("you can't relate sexually to women") may be seen by the client as a matter of value commitment ("I don't want to relate to women sexually; I prefer men"). Who is correct, the counselor or the client? Without resolving the question in this case, it should be enough to make our point; without a context of normative value symbols, value confusion arises and care becomes difficult if not impossible.

Purely from the standpoint of preventive mental health, the minister as a facilitator of a community of moral inquiry can make an enormous contribution. In saying this, let me point out that mental health as such and preventive medicine are not the defining goals of ministry. The mental health professions may sometimes look at the ministry of the church in this fashion. But when they do, they apply *their* categories to ministry rather than viewing ministry within its own self-understanding. The minister is interested primarily in building a moral universe and facilitating right conduct in a community of persons. My point is that to build a moral community is to contribute to health. To help establish the value framework for right action is to contribute indirectly to health. To minimize value confusion, to clarify the objects and values worthy of people's loyalty, is to contribute to their emotional and mental well-being.

In asserting this, I do not suggest that healthy action and moral action are synonymous. Let me state the differences between these concepts rather sharply now and inject some important qualifications later. Healthy action has to do with the capacity to act without conflict. Moral action has to do with the intention to act responsibly so that the consequences of one's action contribute to the enrichment of values for oneself and the wider community. In spite of these differences, health will be increased when the value context of one's actions gains greater clarity. So when the minister, through his preaching and through his work with groups, stimulates a community of moral inquiry not only is he building a moral world, he is caring for the health of both his church members and the larger society which they may influence.

Hence, it is of utmost importance for the minister and the entire congregation to develop a sense of accumulative result. Their moral deliberations should get somewhere. They must develop a sense of tradition—a sense of style. An organic sense of *style*—of the way "we people are"—is fundamental if a community of moral discourse is to become a community of action. Such a style is important if pastoral care is to transcend remedial counseling and become a matter of incorporating people into a moral world that actually commands attention and influences thought and action. In other words, the congregation should develop its own oral and written traditions, equivalent in function to the Midrash, Mishnah, and Talmud. To say this does not mean that these efforts to develop a sense of style would be discontinuous with the traditions of the past. They would use the resources of the past, but they must also involve themselves in appropriating and redefining these traditions to fit the circumstances of today and tomorrow. Neither do I want to convey the idea that the individual church should attempt to develop its own moral style in isolation from the wider church—the denomination to which it belongs and the wider ecumenical church. The wider church must also be a community of moral inquiry. Communication must proceed in both directions between the wider church and the local church. Much of this kind of communication occurs today and it should increase in the future. But the weight of these remarks is the contention that all these levels of moral inquiry contribute directly to the most intimate and mundane aspects of the pastoral care ministry of the local church. They help to create a moral universe, a world of moral meanings—a context for care.

83466

LINCOLN CHRISTIAN COLLEGE AND SEMINARY

MORAL INQUIRY AND RITUAL

It is because the church is a worshiping community that it differs from a forum for debate, a town council, or a legislative body. Through moral inquiry the church attempts to create the value symbols necessary for a religiocultural moral vision. But the church does not simply project these value symbols as abstract ideas and concepts. The church attempts to do what religion everywhere in its worship and ritual attempts to do; that is, it attempts to *embody* these meanings in the minds and hearts of its people.[6] It attempts to make these meanings seem real, concrete, alive, attractive, and commanding. This is the function of ritual repetition. Through dramatic repetition, ritual attempts to deepen within the worshiping community a sense for the solidarity of the value symbols it has come to believe are important.[7] It is the nature of the truly religious community to be afraid of disembodiment, to be skeptical of too great a distance between symbol and embodied action. When this occurs, the religiocultural world seems unsubstantial and ephemeral. Ritual tries to create a world of meaning and give it a sense of permanence through repetition. In the relative isolation of the worshiping situation, the congregation attempts to reenact the essential features of how the world should be. In this way, it further convinces its members of the validity of this vision and deepens their sense for the possibility of it becoming reality.

If this is the function of worship, it is easy to see why worship is so difficult in modern societies. It is more difficult in complex and changing societies to achieve a sense of a stable moral world —a world that worship might further consolidate and deepen in our consciousness. When we see that our moral world is changing, that we ourselves are constructing a slightly different moral world, this sense of transition seems to undermine and relativize the earlier ritually consolidated worlds we had achieved. All of this I am ready to admit; ritual and worship are more difficult in modern societies. There is something innately conservative behind the human hunger for worship. It gives expression to the desire to have permanent meanings able to withstand the transitions and crises of life. This is why the Word is more fundamental than ritual and sacrament. If our thesis is true that the Judeo-Christian conglomerate is primarily an ethical type of religious tradition, then the demands of moral inquiry and moral discourse must take priority over the thirst for ritual settledness. But in reality, there may be resources within Christianity that permit both moral inquiry and ritual enactment to occur if each is properly conceived.

Our thesis is that Christianity adds the dimension of "spiritual existence" to the tradition of practical rationality and moral action characteristic of normative Judaism. Jesus' sense for the in-breaking of the kingdom of God, his conviction that this in-breaking brought forgiveness to all who would receive it, and the early Christians' experience of being empowered by the Spirit of God—these justify for most of the Christian churches the fact that the drama of forgiveness is the central feature of their ritual. If the relationship between forgiveness and moral inquiry is properly understood, it means that Christians should have the courage to pursue vigorously the goals of the moral life with assurance. If they miss the mark, or if they falter, forgiveness is a possibility and through this they can be renewed again to pursue the moral course. Forgiveness makes the moral life possible. It frees us to pursue the moral life with a minimum of stultifying guilt and sense of defeat. But without assuming the seriousness of the demand of Christianity for ethical inquiry and conduct, forgiveness loses its meaning and its renewing power. He who would claim to be a Christian must have been first a Pharisee—at least in spirit. There is no possibility of becoming a Christian except through the narrow passage of the spirit of Pharisaism. It is only against the background of the tenacious concern to define in practical ways and with great attention to detail the meaning of the law that the gospel of forgiveness has power.

Central to ritual in the Christian community should be the dimension of forgiveness. Forgiveness, in fact, is the *invariant* dimension of Christian worship; it is the part of Christian ritual most amenable to repetition. The moral vision that results from moral inquiry is the more variable part of our ritual—the part that changes somewhat to fit the evolving social and cultural situation. The dimension of forgiveness is the more constant part of Christian worship. It is that invariant element which in fact can give the moral inquiry of the Christian a higher degree of flexibility, openness, and potential relevance than ever was the case with the Pharisaic mentality itself. But it must be clear that the affirmation I can give to Pharisaism and Christianity is not due only to their importance for my own religious heritage, although this is indeed important. It is because, in addition, I find philosophical grounds which suggest the validity of these modalities of life for the human species. Man the cultural animal must live by rules and a moral vision. His rules and moral vision can be more responsive to changing circumstances if he also lives by forgiveness. The dialectical context of Christianity is Pharisaism. Without the context of Pharisaism, Christianity becomes pure liminality—communitas without structure, dynamics without form.

How is this relevant to the situation of care in the church? Pastoral care must never be considered as simply a matter of implementing forgiveness even though forgiveness is an essential part of all care.[8] Pastoral care should never be understood simply as a matter of "loosening people up," helping them to become "more open" or more "spontaneous and flexible," "removing their guilt," or making them "more loving." Nor is pastoral care ever just a matter of "relativizing" another person's assumptions, character structure, cultural values, etc., although at times these emphases are important. Pastoral care must first be concerned to give a person a structure, a character, an identity, a religiocultural value system out of which to live. It must first be concerned to help people discover these things and become incorporated into them. Then it should concern itself with the issues of forgiveness, guilt, and related emotional-dynamic issues connected with actually attempting to live the life that moral inquiry has found to be good.

All of this means that the preoccupation with therapeutic acceptance and Christian forgiveness characteristic of the 1960's, especially the work of Paul Tillich, Seward Hiltner, Daniel Day Williams, Thomas Oden, and myself was not so much wrong as one-sided in its emphasis. Much of this work failed to place its theologies of acceptance fully within a context of practical moral rationality such as was characteristic of the Hebrew backgrounds to primitive Christianity. It tended to see things as either/or. It tended to see Pharisaic moral scrupulosity as one thing and Christian forgiveness as something else. It is now my contention that the two belong together. Christianity grew out of the vigorous and practical moral rationality of scribal Judaism and therefore necessarily assumes this as its dialectical context. For instance, to put it bluntly in another context—the context of anomic and rapidly changing Western society—Christianity stripped of its Jewish context can easily give rise to moral absurdities.

CARE AND COUNSELING

My task has been to set forth the hierarchy of the church's care. To do this, I have first characterized the church as a community of moral inquiry, discourse, and action. But in contrast to other such communities, the church self-consciously attempts to give ritual articulation to the moral universe that it constructs. Religion everywhere resorts to ritual. This is the major difference between religion and philosophy or religion and rational ethics. But in a so-called secular society, religion does not disappear, it simply becomes more diffuse, more unselfconscious, more informal, and less structured in its manifestations. Other communities besides the church are involved in moral inquiry and ritual. For instance, take the university. Certainly moral inquiry is a part of the work of the university. Those of us who pursue vocations in the context of the university certainly know that it has its rituals. On the whole, moral inquiry is not the major goal of the university as it exists today. More frequently the intention of rendering visible the way things *are,* rather than how they *should* be, constitutes the major preoccupation of the university. If moral inquiry and moral discourse occupy a portion of the interest of the university, it seldom believes its task to include actually attempting to give embodiment to the results of its inquiry. The university is a specialized institution—highly important for complex technological societies such as our own. It is more interested in the true than the good, in thought and inquiry than action, in the rituals necessary to maintain its life than the ritual repetition of the vision of the world it deems good. On the other hand, the church is interested in all these dimensions. It is interested in moral inquiry and action. It is interested as much in the good as in the true. And it seeks to give ritual expression not only to its own maintenance but to the larger view of the good world that it projects.

There is no justifiable way of speaking about the care performed by the church unless one envisions this care in the *context* of an inquiring and worshiping church. The fundamental ambiguity of much that is called pastoral care today is exactly its tendency to perceive itself as an activity independent of or somehow not fundamentally influenced by this context. This is especially true of much that goes by the name of "pastoral counseling." This situation has arisen for two reasons. The first is due to the rise of centers of specialized pastoral counseling which often have only a remote relationship either to the local church or to larger denominational and ecumenical expressions of the church. The other reason is the fruitful but somewhat uncritical borrowing from models of secular psychotherapy as a resource for pastoral care and counseling within the church. One hears of various types of pastoral counseling occurring, such as Rogerian pastoral counseling, Jungian pastoral counseling, transactional analysis pastoral counseling, Gestalt pastoral counseling, rational-emotive pastoral counseling, etc. Books and articles are being written about pastoral counseling from these perspectives. Generally, however, one discovers that the controlling and defining dimension about these forms of counseling is the secular name attached to them —Rogers, transactional analysis, gestalt—and not anything that is indeed pastoral about this counseling.

Let us assume the context of the church. Let us assume further that pastoral care is primarily a matter of facilitating a mode of inquiry that will help the members of the church to develop a framework of meanings relevant to all aspects of their lives. Then what is the role of pastoral counseling as such? To answer this question, I will first attempt to distinguish between pastoral care as moral inquiry and pastoral care as counseling. Pastoral care as moral inquiry attempts to keep moral concerns uppermost in conversations and deliberations with individuals and members of a church. On the other hand, pastoral counseling to some extent brackets moral issues and focuses more specifically on emotional-dynamic issues that block persons from living the kind of life they hope for and believe in.

The distinction between pastoral care as moral inquiry and pastoral care as counseling should never be absolute. It has been the great contribution of psychiatry and psychology to demonstrate to us that the human will is not free to follow under all circumstances the dictates and values of our consciences. Although in various ways our theological heritage recognized the conditionedness and captivity of the will, the modern psychological sciences have deepened and particularized our sensitivity to this aspect of the human condition. This is why, even in the context of pastoral care as moral inquiry, the minister should be sensitive to how difficult it is for various persons freely to inquire into the nature of the good and freely to adhere to what their own inquiry suggests. So, in the context of the moral inquiry groups that have so much to do with forming the moral style of the congregation, the minister—and others—should try to develop a profound sensitivity to the emotional-dynamic conflicts that people bring to this inquiry. The very process of moral discourse is indeed difficult for some people.

On the other hand, in pastoral care as counseling, the bracketing of moral issues should never be absolute. Insofar as the minister is counseling someone who is a member of his church, that person should himself be a part of the broader moral inquiry which goes on in that church. In other words, he will know where the minister and the church stand on a variety of issues. And even though in the process of their pastoral conversations, the minister and the troubled person might never address explicitly issues of moral meaning, such meanings would constitute an assumed horizon to all that they discuss. There will be times when the minister and the troubled person will discuss directly these moral issues which constitute the background of meaning for the particular problems that the person is having. But when they do this, the conversation has not left its basic focus on the emotional and dynamic issues that have led to the person's conflicts and difficulties.

Let me be more direct. Let me assert emphatically that the minister needs, upon occasion, to have the luxury to bracket moral issues from the focus of his pastoral conversations. There are times when the dynamic issues must be in the forefront—even of pastoral conversations. But he can only earn this luxury when he has already been to some extent successful in his primary task of stimulating a community of moral inquiry that is constructing the positive meanings that will function in the lives of his congregation.

At this level of pastoral counseling, the minister also should be free to employ any of the other group methods, such as T-groups, sensitivity groups, or encounter groups, that he finds useful. It is at this level that the discussion should go on as to whether TA is better than gestalt, Rogerianism better than Freudianism, or Jung better than any of them. All these therapies, quasi therapies, and growth groups are basically useful at the level of increasing a person's ability to be free to act. On the whole, these various psychological methods do not address directly issues dealing with the nature of the morally good. On the whole, they enable a person to increase the range of his freedom. They do not address directly what a person should do with his freedom. In view of this, the preoccupation of both pastoral counseling specialists and ministers of local churches with the techniques of counseling, and with the relative merits of the several approaches and methods, show only how far removed most of pastoral counseling is from what should be the real heart of pastoral care.

This is not to say that it is irrelevant to discuss which of the practical psychologies can best be used in the context of a community of moral inquiry and action. In fact, this is an extremely important question, both at the level of practice and at the level of the religiocultural vision to which the church subscribes. It may be that some of the psychotherapeutic psychologies entail views of man and of the world which are in strong contradiction to the visions that undergird the idea of a worshiping community of moral inquiry. This may not be any great problem if these psychologies are used primarily as techniques designed to handle specific dynamic issues in counseling. But such a neat distinction between the culture of these therapies and the central religiocultural vision of the church is seldom possible. In fact, as I indicated in the Introduction, the cultures of these psychotherapeutic techniques can often become inflated and take on the characteristics of religious myth. Ministers begin to quote Fritz Perls, Thomas Harris, Rollo May, or Carl Jung in their sermons. Efforts to correlate Perls, Rogers, Jung, or Freud with Christianity occur. The symbol system of the Judeo-Christian conglomerate begins to be interpreted with the perspective of certain psychotherapeutic psychologies. Laymen begin to read the books of these writers more frequently than they do the writings of theologians. The various mass media popularize such views and the related vocabulary. People begin to talk about their experience in the jargon of these therapies. We speak of giving each other "strokes," of reading our own and other persons' "scripts," of "owning our feelings," of "being open," of "free associating," and of "accepting" one another. All this can happen among persons who have never experienced a counseling relationship or been in an encounter group. It is good to review, analyze, and critique the various psychological theories, but for cultural reasons—reasons of faith, ideology, and religiocultural vision—as much as for reasons of technique and psychotherapeutic power.

I will restate the hierarchy of care as I have discussed it so far. There is a place in the church for pastoral counseling of all kinds

—counseling with the sick and bereaved, one-to-one counseling, group counseling, encounter groups, growth groups, etc.—as long as they are placed firmly within a context of a community of moral inquiry. The minister has a clear duty to counsel the ill and dying, but he should first have helped create a community with a religiocultural view of the meaning of illness and death. Certainly the minister should counsel persons with marriage problems, sexual problems, and divorce problems, but he should first have helped to create among his people a positive vision of the normative meaning of marriage, sexuality, and even divorce. The difficulty with much of pastoral counseling today is that more time is spent discussing the tools of counseling than in the more challenging process of developing the structure of meanings that should constitute the context for counseling.

In other words, pastoral counseling must be founded on a context of moral meanings that is, in fact, the province of practical theology. Practical theology is a branch of theology that attempts to state explicitly the ultimate grounds upon which we shall order the everyday moral meanings of our lives. It has a close relationship with theological ethics. It is different from fundamental theology, which attempts to explain the ultimate grounds and justifications for the basic symbols of a particular religious tradition. Fundamental theology, in the case of Christianity, would consist of the legitimation of the truth of such basic symbols as God, Christ, creation, and salvation. Practical theology builds on fundamental theology, but goes farther. It demonstrates the meaning of these basic symbols for the ordering of daily life. In addition, I would distinguish practical theology from pastoral theology. Pastoral theology attempts to set forth the legitimations for specific pastoral acts—the minister's preaching, liturgical duties, pastoral care, and pastoral counseling. Practical theology goes beyond a theology of pastoral acts and sets forth a theology of practical living—a theology of work, business, sexuality, marriage, child-rearing, aging, youth, etc. Practical theology in this sense of the word is the most neglected of any of the specialties of theology.

CARE AND THE COUNSELING SPECIALIST

One of the most important movements within the ministry of
the Christian church in recent years is the appearance of the
specialized pastoral counselor. He can be found in a variety of
places—in a hospital chaplaincy, in a pastoral counseling center,
as a part of the ministry of a local congregation, or sometimes in
private practice. Regardless of where the specialized pastoral
counselor is found, his work is somewhat removed from the wide
range of pastoral acts that the congregational minister performs.
Most specifically, his work is removed from the central task of
developing a community of moral inquiry and action.

The distance of the specialized counselor from the direct process of moral discourse is intentional and necessary. People go to
the specialist for two reasons. First, their problems at the emotional-dynamic level are too complex for the congregational minister to handle and still give sufficient attention to his other duties.
Second, some persons without particularly complex emotional
difficulties want the leisure to improve and grow in their emotional skills. In both cases, the emotional-dynamic issues are in
the forefront and moral concerns are rightly in the background.
In the sociology of Talcott Parsons, we can find a powerful justification for the specialized pastoral counselor. It is the minister's
primary task to help establish and maintain the moral vision of
the worshiping community and the wider society. This compro-
mises his ability to go far in prolonged and highly time-consum-
ing counseling relationships, which by definition entail some
bracketing of moral concerns.[9] On the other hand, the person who
wants to disentangle his emotional involvements or who wants
the leisure to grow in his emotional capacity, needs just the kind
of bracketing of moral questions that the minister can indulge in
only up to a point. Therefore, *there is a legitimate role for the
specialized pastoral counselor.*

But if, by definition, the specialized counselor should enjoy
some distance (qua counselor) from the direct concerns of moral

inquiry, what then makes his counseling pastoral? What does he bring that cannot be brought by the social worker, the psychologist, the psychoanalyst? There are two levels at which this question can be answered. The first level has been most popular in recent years. It says that there is something intrinsically religious —perhaps even Christian—in the quality of the psychotherapeutic relationships offered by almost any counselor. This religious quality is the "acceptance," or "unconditioned positive regard," that is present in nearly all counseling relationships and that permits counselees to relax, open up, and investigate their feelings. Theological inquiries into psychotherapy by Paul Tillich, Daniel Day Williams, Thomas Oden, and myself have tried to clarify the religious and theological dimension of this level of meaning. From this point of view, the difference between the secular psychotherapist and the pastoral counseling specialist is that the latter is *conscious* that his acceptance of the counselee is grounded in a deeper structure of meaning which undergirds all acceptance and love, i.e., the acceptance and love of God. It follows from this that the secular counselor is unconscious or for some reason oblivious to the fact that his therapeutic acceptance has such a transcendent meaning. In terms of the two-dimensional theory of the sacred put forth in these chapters, therapeutic acceptance is functionally equivalent to the liminal or communitas moment of the therapeutic process.

There is another way of distinguishing between the secular psychotherapist and the pastoral counseling specialist. This second method has to do with the issue of *context*. The moral context of the specialized pastoral counselor—whether he works in a congregation, a center, or a hospital—should be fairly visible both to members of the Christian church and to the wider public. The explicitness of the moral vision implicit in his institutional context is a crucial characteristic of the specialized pastoral counselor that distinguishes him from the secular counseling specialist.

On the basis of the value commitments publicly affirmed by the institutions that legitimate the pastoral specialist, the counselor's moral commitments on a variety of issues will be easy to surmise, especially on those issues generally pertinent to the personal problems for which people seek counseling. When a person goes to a pastoral counseling specialist, that person should have some sense of where the counselor stands on such moral issues as the nature and organization of the family, the relations of the sexes, race relations, the nature of social justice, the morality of divorce, and many others. All specialized pastoral counseling should be able to show how it enjoys the sanction of the larger church. In addition, the value assumptions of the wider church should surround the religiocultural background of the specialized counseling situation. If this wider religiocultural context of the specialized pastoral counselor cannot be assumed, if for some reason it is confused, vague, or not clear in the mind of church members and the wider secular community, then both the church and the pastoral specialist must work to make it open and intelligible to both groups. When the value assumptions of the pastoral counseling specialist are relatively clear, *then they can be bracketed.* When the counselor can assume—because of his institutional context—that the client is reasonably clear about what the counselor's value commitments are, then the counselor can with good conscience set them aside and concentrate on emotional-dynamic issues without the fear that in the process he will be unwittingly confirming a value structure that the counselor does not believe in. On the other hand—and this is even more important—when the client is reasonably certain about the outlines of the counselor's value system, the client can in good faith bracket value issues. He can look at emotional-dynamic issues without fearing that in the process of gaining insight into his emotional conflicts, he is unwittingly being inducted into a set of values that he does not know, does not consciously affirm, and cannot subscribe to.

Hence it is of the highest importance for the specialized pastoral counselor and the wider church to remain in active communication. There is communication now, but it is too narrow to fulfill what needs to be accomplished. Most of the communication between church and pastoral specialist has to do with what the pastoral specialist can teach the congregational minister about handling troubled persons. This is good and important. But the conversation also should flow the other way. The pastoral counseling specialist and the wider church should pool their insights and experience in an effort to clarify where the church actually stands on some of the vital value issues that confront the church and intimately affect the counseling situation. Such issues as the meaning of marriage, alternatives to marriage, women's liberation, the meaning of retirement, and the meaning of money are examples of questions that the church and the specialized pastoral counselor should define in active dialogue.

Yet this does not appear to be happening. The majority of those who make up the American Association of Pastoral Counselors and the Association for Clinical Pastoral Education are becoming more and more preoccupied with issues relating to counseling techniques and less and less interested as professionals in issues related to ethics, theology, and the philosophy of religion. I have never heard of a conversation, panel, or task force involving these pastoral specialists and the larger church that was designed to address one of the major value issues facing our society today—the resolution of which, if reached, would be publicly announced and form the value context of specialized pastoral counseling. Pastoral specialists connected with general hospitals are beginning to realize that their work with individuals and small groups must be informed by a more explicit value context. Especially is this true in the area of medical experimentation, organ transplants, and the entire field of medical intervention in borderline cases of birth, aging, and death.

But the pastoral counseling specialists in other situations generally seem unaware that their counseling should proceed in a fairly clear value context. Because of the general sociological situation this value context is becoming more and more unclear to persons both in and out of the church. In order to be able, during counseling, to give his clients a "sanctioned vacation" from the religiocultural values that should rule their everyday lives, the specialized counselor must himself help build and main-

tain the value context that he so adroitly brackets in counseling
situations. Only by being directly involved in creating and maintaining this religiocultural value framework can the counselor
call himself "pastoral." Only because he knows how to relax its
demands and concentrate on emotional-dynamic issues has he the
right to call himself a "counseling specialist."

CIVILIZATION AND CARE

I have set forth a hierarchical model of pastoral care. I have
associated care with the process of constructing a world of moral
meanings and helping persons become a part of this world. This
obviously associates pastoral care with the historic functions of
pastoral discipline more than has been the case in recent years by
many prominent Protestant theorists. Yet, as John McNeill has
pointed out, throughout the history of the church, pastoral care
has been primarily pastoral discipline.[10] If there is a difference
between the model that I have suggested and these historic traditions, it is that there is more emphasis on helping people to create
and subscribe to a moral world rather than on ways of punishing
and correcting people when they fall away from that world. The
point of view developed here assumes that our moral world in
modern society is unstable to begin with. When that is the case,
the emphasis can never be on punishment alone. The issues at
stake in this discussion transcend the parochial concerns of the
Christian church and the maintenance of its life and services. It
is my argument that it is the function of religion in any society
to create the highest levels of the symbolic meaning and value
which govern that society. The church is an explicitly religious
institution; if it does not perform this function for society, some
other institution or movement will. There are religious and quasi-
religious forces in Western society other than the institutional
church which aspire to compete with it and replace its influence.
If this actually is happening, then these new forces will have to
play the role that the churches once played. I have only attempted
to reveal some of the resources that I believe the Judeo-Christian

conglomerate has for continuing to play this role of creating and maintaining an ethical structure for culture. But whether the churches do this or whether other forces do it, the fact remains that the counseling specialist—secular or religious—functions in a religiocultural context and that this context is of crucial significance for his work. Without the recognition of this truth, all counseling and psychotherapy will have an anticultural or culturally destructive influence on the rest of society. Specialized counseling, both inside and outside the church, may be failing to recognize the validity of this observation. It may in fact be undermining the idea of culture.

VI

Method in Religious Living

For various reasons, it seems unnatural to bring up the question of method in religious living. It creates images of medieval Catholic monks saying prayers in their narrow cells in the darkness of the early morning, of Christian ascetics fasting to gain control of their passions, or of elderly ladies having devotions—all in a circle. Yet students of religion know that where there is religion, there is method for living the religious life. Prayer, liturgy, meditation, ascetic disciplines, mutual confessions, koans, the systematic study of sacred writings, and other such practices are found wherever religions are found.

The Neglect of Method in Religious Living

But we have grown accustomed to ignoring the supporting methods designed to deepen and consolidate the religious life. Now the question arises, what are the preferred methods of the Christian? How do we implement our faith and regularize our lives? Is it by prayer, meditation, confession, fasting? All of these, or none of these? Is one method more crucial than another? I will not disparage any of these familiar methods, but I will point to a method that I believe has been overlooked as fundamental to the Christian life.

Since the time of the Reformation, Protestantism has had grounds for suspecting method in the context of the religious life.

Method can sound like "works," and works easily calls to mind the onerous phrase "justification by works." Justification by grace was the sole ground for salvation in normative Reformation theology. To speak of method in religious living seems to suggest what the individual can "do" to improve his religious life. What the individual can "do" suggests "works," and "works" flies in the face of *sola fide* and *sola gratia.*

Many ministers and theologians of this generation cut their theological teeth on neo-Reformation theology. We too have been suspicious of salvation by "works." In accord with our Pauline heritage we have been vigilant against legalism and moralism. Under the influence of insights from psychoanalysis, we have become skeptical of compulsiveness, obsessiveness, and rigidity. We have assumed that, where there are fixed schedules, rigid patterns, repetitive practices, and regular disciplines, there we could be sure that man's gravest sin—his indomitable tendency to save himself—is asserting itself once again. When neo-Reformation theology and psychoanalysis formed a kind of cultural alliance (clinical pastoral education and pastoral psychotherapy are symbols of this alliance), the educated minister more or less accepted Freud's theory about the relationship of obsessive practices and religious ritual.[1] Both, it was thought, are a result of repression. Of course, neither the Protestant minister nor the pastoral counseling specialist completely accepted this equation. But gradually they did tend to associate healthy religion with spontaneity and spontaneity with grace and faith. To speak of method in religious living was to conjure up a long list of negative associations—justification by works, sin, legalism, moralism, obsessiveness, and compulsiveness. On the other hand, method in religious living was suspect because it could serve as an *obstacle* to grace.

My concerns will be clearer if I point out the drastic decline in practical supports for religious living that occurred at the time of the Protestant Reformation. The ancient Jew had the law. More accurately he had a method for practical moral rationality and moral decision-making which, as Max Weber has suggested,

was probably unique on the face of the earth. Even though the
early Christians relativized somewhat the Jewish legal tradition,
it was still very much a part of their assumptive world. In addition, the Christians who were addressed in the Pauline letters
gathered in small groups to practice what John McNeill has
called "mutual edification" and "fraternal correction." The
Christians of the second century developed systems of public
confession and penance. These systems were amplified by the
great penitential codes of the Middle Ages. Private confession and
penance replaced the practice of public confession of the second,
third, and fourth centuries. The penitentials and their systems of
confession and penance were the great medieval methods for
supporting the religious life.

But with the coming of the Reformation, most of these supports to the religious life disappeared. Gone was the support of
the oral legal tradition of late Old Testament Judaism. Gone for
a while were the practices of mutual edification and fraternal
correction of early Christianity. And gone were the penitentials
and their systems of public and private confession. In their place
were a man's naked conscience and his direct prayerful relationship to his God. It is true that in the left-wing Reformation
groups and in Methodism, small-group edification and correction
were practiced, but in the twentieth century, even these practices
languished.

WHERE DO WE TURN
FOR METHOD IN RELIGIOUS LIVING?

The issue of method in religious living is arising again. Theologians of the last forty years have restored to the faithful Protestant a sense of grace and forgiveness, but modern theologians
have had little to say about a self-sustaining method for religious
living. It was assumed that once the Christian felt the experience
of grace and forgiveness, he would spontaneously know what to
do, how to act, and how to put his life together in the context of
our highly pluralistic and rapidly changing society. This assump-

tion may have been wrong. It is probably not that simple. In addition, certain currents among the laity of the church and within the larger society suggest that this point of view was naïve and mistaken.

The phenomenon of identity confusion both within and outside the church may point to the failure of this vacuum in practical method. In a pluralistic and rapidly changing society where value options are myriad, we are struck by the instability of commitment and self-definition that characterizes wide sectors of the population, even the laity and ministers of the churches. In addition, our laity—and especially our youth—are reaching out and grasping things that seem strange and even bizarre. We are surprised that while mainline theologians characterize our society as secular, our youth have been flocking back to fundamentalism, flirting with esoteric Eastern religions, and attaching themselves to gurus who can teach them the technologies of self-control and self-transcendence.

Second, the phenomenal growth of the encounter group movement should indicate how hungry people are for practical methods for living. Most of these groups are presented as growth groups rather than therapeutic groups, even if, as Morton Lieberman and others have demonstrated, they are often far more psychotherapeutically oriented than they admit.[2] Kurt Back, in his provocative book entitled *Beyond Words,* has argued that the encounter group movement has quasi-religious dimensions; it helps to satisfy some of the needs of a "loved-starved" and rootless people in a highly mobile and transient society.[3] My colleague David Orlinsky has expressed the belief that many of these groups gather around them a wider community of persons who attempt to apply in their daily living the techniques, styles of analysis, and methods of self-manipulation which they have learned in these groups.[4] It may be possible that ministers and pastoral counseling specialists have also contributed to the belief that not only do such theorists as Carl Rogers, Fritz Perls, Eric Berne, or William Schutz have important contributions to make to the specific situation of counseling, but they also have something to contribute to the process of religious living in general.

But the newest and most sensational evidence of the thirst for method is the recent interest, especially among the young, in the meditational psychologies of the East and the scientific discoveries about the psychology of meditation that have occurred in the United States in the last ten years.[5] Pastoral counseling specialists may talk about the superiority of Perls or Berne, Rogers or Skinner. But many of the young in our colleges and universities are talking about whether it is hatha-yoga or kundalini, satipatthana or mahamudra, Zen or transcendental meditation. It is not the psychologies of interpersonal enrichment that they seek. It is the psychologies of altered states of consciousness which excite them and impel them to further inquiry. These psychologies promise to provide many Westerners with new methods of introspective analysis and new methods of internal control over both autonomic and central nervous system processes and over systems controlled by both the left and the right hemispheres of the brain.[6]

WILL ANY METHOD DO?

So, in an effort to protect the sovereignty and initiative of God, Protestant theologians tended to neglect the matter of method in religious living. But the broad mass of human beings are different; they will have their methods—their technologies to control their passions, order their identities, and induce their yearning for ecstatic experience. What does this mean for the person who identifies with the Judeo-Christian tradition? And what does it mean for ministers who should try to meet people's needs for some kind of method for religious living? Does it mean that all methods are equal, just as all psychotherapies are equal, as long as they produce equally enthusiastic testimony from those who resort to them?

What will be our criteria of selection? After devouring approximately seven different waves of psychotherapeutic technique within the last twenty years, should the minister and pastoral specialist take a new step and absorb the new psychologies of meditation? These new psychologies not only promise to deliver the mystical tradition of the East, they also promise to restore the mystical traditions of the West—not only kundalini but Thomas a Kempis, not only Zen but Teresa of Avila as well.

I am quite convinced that the old and new psychologies of meditation will soon burst forth upon the pastoral psychology movement—upon the pastoral counseling specialist as well as the clinical pastoral educator. With the physically sick, the dying, the mentally confused, the grieving; with ourselves, our students, and our parishioners, it is most likely that within a relatively short time we will be using these new methods. Still, I am reluctant to say that these new meditational approaches should constitute the heart of what I have been referring to under the rubric of method in religious living. They may indeed appropriately be the heart of religious living as it has taken shape in the East. They have certainly played a role at certain crucial moments in the Judeo-Christian tradition of the West. But I submit that there is a deeper core, a more abiding element, that might offer the key to method to those of us who locate ourselves in this tradition.

METHOD IN THE
JUDEO-CHRISTIAN TRADITION

I embark upon this subject with some hesitation. In an effort to locate the meaning of method in the Judeo-Christian context, I fear that I will appear to be reverting back to the long list of negatives I referred to earlier. I have no wish to revive justification by works, law, legalism, obsessiveness, compulsiveness, moralism, and rigidity. But I am going to argue that there is an essential element of this religious tradition which we are neglecting. This element has great implications for method in religious living within both Judaism and Christianity, in spite of the important differences between these two traditions. The element that I am holding up for reconsideration is the *core* of Judaism and the *context* of Christianity. In the contemporary situation, both Christianity and Judaism are giving scant attention to it. Although it is not the core of Christianity, the element that I have in mind is so absolutely essential to this religious tradition that without its vigorous presence, Christianity degenerates into amorphous ambiguity and cultural chaos.

What is this mysterious element that I have in mind? It is the system of practical moral rationality practiced first by the Levites and later by the scribes and Pharisees of ancient Judaism. In selecting this as a unique element in Judaism and an essential contextual background to Christianity, I follow the comparative sociology of religion of Max Weber. In Weber's monumental *Ancient Judaism,* he makes the point that the unique feature of Judaism in comparison with other religions of the ancient world was the Levitical system of practical moral rationality built around the interpretation and implementation of the covenant law.[7] It should be of special interest to both the minister and the pastoral counseling specialist to note that all of this went on, according to Weber, in the context of practices in the cure of souls. It was primarily in the context of the pastoral care of the individual—probably including princes, kings, and other politically powerful persons—that this system of practical rationality was first introduced into Hebrew life.

Why does Weber call this process of interpreting the covenant law to troubled individuals and casuistically extending it to new situations practical rationality? The answer is that it replaced guidance of individuals by magic, oracle, and the drawing of lots —typical methods of guidance in the ancient world. Guidance of individuals by the law required knowledge of the moral law, not mystical or esoteric gnosis as possessed by the Indian Brahman. It was *practical* because the knowledge involved was not a dispassionate quest for abstract truth as idealized in later Greek philosophy. It was a knowledge designed to guide action, practice, and conduct. It had real elements of rationality because it was alive, entailed interpretation, and was adapted to changing circumstances.

In later Judaism, but still before the time of Jesus, the instruction, interpretation, and casuistic amplification of the covenant law became a primary concern of noncultic groups of teachers called scribes and Pharisees. The passion of the Pharisee was to take the law to the people, to give the average man direct access to the law, and to make out of Israel a "nation of priests." Although they probably were overzealous at times and thereby became an object of the critical reaction of both Jesus and Paul, the practical rationality of the Pharisees was far more liberal, far more flexible, and far more dynamic for its day than we often have been led to think. Biblical scholars, especially W. D. Davies, tell us that it was the Sadducees, not the Pharisees, who were the traditionalists and the conservatives. By being literalists with regard to the law of Moses, the more priestly Sadducees made the law irrelevant to the novel circumstances of their day. Davies writes:

> The essence of Pharisaism is the belief that religion covers the whole of life. . . . This meant that for the Pharisee it was possible by the examination, exposition, and adaptation of the text of the Law to find what was the right conduct and to prescribe it for every circumstance in life. This seems to have been the Pharisaic ideal, the creation of a community governed by a code which provided a detailed chart which could be variously applied. They were the progressives. . . . The method by which they sought to do this is preserved for us, probably in broad outlines in the Misnah.[8]

What was this method? Davies is correct when he says that the best insight into how they proceeded might come from the codification of the oral tradition in the Mishnah, which occurred at least a hundred years after the death of Jesus. Jacob Neusner's invaluable book entitled *Invitation to the Talmud,* although dealing with these later documents, doubtless gives insight into methods of practical moral rationality that obtained even in postexilic Judaism. It was a method of mutual criticism that emphasized the importance of publicly articulated reasons for moral action.[9] The authority of the past was acknowledged, but it was not the ultimate authority. As Neusner writes, "What counts is reason, ubiquitous, predominant, penetrating."[10] It was not the authority of

ancient rabbis themselves which counted, but the "timeless, im-
personal reasons for ruling as they did."[11] Through the development of rules that were commonly shared but that were always
open to criticism and refinement, impulse was regulated and directed but not repressed. The asceticism of the Pharisee and the
rabbi who followed him was a positive asceticism; there was a
high evaluation of man's appetites, but an equally strong emphasis on their appropriate regulation.

This tradition of practical moral rationality is relevant for our
religious living today and may have something to contribute to
our various models of training for pastoral care and counseling.
The argument I am developing is a formal one. I am not saying
that the law of the Levitical priest or the Pharisee can be the law
for us in any simple sense. Nor will I argue that, because Jesus
was born out of this tradition, for this reason alone, it has a special
claim upon us. My argument is more philosophical. But it is
relevant to point out that Jesus, in spite of his differences with the
Pharisees, was seen by his contemporaries as a teacher and a rabbi
who was closely associated with the style and concerns of the
Pharisaic tradition. Although much of Jesus' ministry was involved with destructuring, simplifying, or intensifying the law, it
is still clear that his ministry presupposed the law and was seen
by him as a fulfillment of it.

It is quite clear that Jesus added something to this tradition of
practical moral rationality. He added a new perception of the
coming of the kingdom of God. No longer was the coming of the
kingdom dependent on the perfect fulfillment of the law as it was
generally thought to be throughout most of ancient Judaism.
Jesus saw the kingdom as inevitable. Perfect obedience to the law
would neither force nor delay its coming. Not only was the kingdom coming, but it was in part already here mediating forgiveness
and grace to all those who would accept it. Therefore, although
there is a sense in which the coming of the kingdom both trans-
forms and transcends any given state of the law, it very much was
thought to fulfill the inner meaning of the law.

But my main point is not primarily hermeneutical with regard to the final relation of law and gospel. It is more simple, primarily philosophical, and possibly even psychological. *Everything that happens in the Gospels presupposes the tradition of practical moral rationality which characterized the existential style of Judaism and the contextual background of the New Testament events.* Let me say it as radically and provocatively as possible. We cannot be Christians without first being Jews, or more accurately, without knowing the method of the Jew. We cannot understand the meaning of forgiveness unless we first throw ourselves into a radical concern about the nature of right moral action. We cannot be delivered from the curse of the law unless first of all we know, contemplate, and strive to keep the law. We cannot comprehend acceptance and grace unless we have first felt the intensity of the Jewish experience of God's command to fulfill the law. If the preaching of the good news of forgiveness and the coming of the kingdom is the unique dimension of Christianity, that uniqueness loses all its meaning when it is not held in the closest tension with the tradition of practical moral rationality of its Jewish context.

BROADER CONSIDERATIONS

Let me conclude by discussing some of the basic reasons why practical methods of moral and ethical deliberations should be introduced into our methods for religious living. The first reason, and the most powerful for the person who is identified with the Christian tradition, is the need to be faithful to the heart of this religion. Christianity was born out of Judaism, and to move Christianity too far from its birthplace is to rob it of a vital dimension. But in asserting this, one must quickly say that to develop a style of practical moral rationality cannot mean the same thing for the twentieth-century Christian as it did for the ancient Jew. Although there were universal elements in the ancient law, the needs of our social existence are vastly different. To be faithful to our Jewish heritage is not necessarily to be faithful to the specifics of its law. Rather it means to be faithful to its appreciation for the need for moral rules, even though in our rapidly changing society these rules must be flexible and constantly under review. This is precisely what the dimensions of forgiveness and grace add to the practical moral rationality of the Jew: they give us the freedom to be morally serious, to face the inevitability of moral mistakes, to sin, and at the same time to recover and revise our moral rules when necessary.

Yet the need to be faithful to the inner core of the Judeo-Christian tradition only has obligatory weight with the person who consciously affirms that tradition. The personal testimony of the believing person is seldom sufficient to convince another individual. Therefore, I want to go farther and set my argument within a philosophical framework.

This leads to the second reason why our methods of religious living need to be informed by methods of practical moral rationality. On philosophical grounds it is possible to argue that man is incurably religious. Furthermore, it is possible to argue philosophically that religions with an ethical impulse—that allow for the efficacy of free moral action—are higher than religions that fail to emphasize this possibility. Both these assertions are worth further consideration.

It is possible to state how humans are incurably religious on anthropological grounds. Man is the creature of instinctual plasticity who cannot find orientation to his world solely on the basis of bodily needs and tendencies. It is clear that the human body is regulated by a variety of patterns, regularities, and rhythms that are crucial for adaptation. But these instinctive and bodily processes are never enough for man to secure a viable relation to his environment.[12] Man is the creature who also needs cognitive symbols, myths, and world views that provide him with a rather encompassing framework of orientation to his world. Man is condemned to live a cognitive existence; he requires symbol systems that give him an interpretative handle on his world. Without these, he becomes disoriented and anxious. Religion provides human beings with these interpretative handles on experience. Man is incurably religious, and if one system of religious symbols seems inadequate, man will seek out or devise another.

Because man is incurably religious, it is better for his religion to contain within it a vision of the importance of responsible and free moral action. Not all religions emphasize this idea. Most religions have systems of ethical codes, but this does not mean that they also emphasize the importance of responsible individual action which is believed to make a difference to the quality of human life. It has been my argument that both Judaism and Christianity are religions of an ethical type and that, to varying degrees, they emphasize this principle.

Why is a religion that offers an ethical vision of the world higher than one that does not? Couldn't it be argued that a religion which deemphasizes individual responsible action and tries to create simple conformity to a given set of rules would actually produce more social harmony? Once again, we must resort to an argument based on a particular understanding of human nature. Most people will admit that human beings are social creatures and must live in some kind of community. In addition, communities need widely shared rules and principles to unify their common life. Yet, the society where each individual accepts responsibility for living by these shared rules will have more flexibility, more capacity to remain alert to changing circumstances, and more capacity for self-correction than the society which deemphasizes individual responsibility. Religions of an ethical type are more serviceable to the human enterprise because they help societies formed by them to develop both firmness and flexibility in handling the vicissitudes of existence.

All the more reason, then, if we are going to be religious and have some method to our living, that it should contain within it a place for practical moral rationality. This is true for those who want to be faithful to their Judeo-Christian heritage. It is true also for those who want to be faithful to the nature of man.

Third, it is important to introduce into our quest for method in religious living ways of practical moral reflection because of the contemporary sociocultural situation. Our present sociocultural situation is one of considerable instability at the level of values. Normative values and value symbols in a society of rapid social change are constantly under enormous strain. The difficulties in developing a stable value context in advanced technological societies has the greatest consequences for individual and corporate well-being. Unless ways are discovered to help individuals and families stabilize their value commitments while values in society are fluid, the rate of emotional illness, identity confusion, and general spiritual malaise will increase alarmingly. It was in an effort to point out this situation that Karl Menninger wrote his book *Whatever Became of Sin?*[13] Menninger and other psychiatrists now are admitting what should be obvious—that the mental health of a people depends on their having resources and methods for making value decisions. Without this, they will sink into a morass of value confusion that inevitably will manifest itself in emotional conflict and general disease. Menninger's book was addressed primarily to ministers with the implicit message that they may have overidentified with the mental health professions and failed to be as forceful as they should be in creating and maintaining viable value symbols to guide everyday life. The book also maintains that unless the psychiatrist and psychologist can assume a more or less usable set of values guiding our practical living, the work of these professionals goes adrift. Mental health professionals can help set people back on a way of life from which they have fallen. It is more than society can demand of these overly burdened professionals to ask them both to set people back on these paths and to *create* the paths in the first place.

The fourth reason has to do with certain ominous trends in contemporary society. Western societies, especially the United States, are almost in a state of panic over the degree of social disintegration that is occurring. The indices can be seen in the sad statistics about crime, addiction, divorce, alcoholism, and mental illness. American society appears to be falling apart at the seams. Debate over this possibility should not obscure the more important danger. Many people are so distraught about the present state of affairs that they are ready to place their trust in almost any firm leadership which will offer them security and order. As Erich Fromm and others have so perceptively pointed out, this is the social environment out of which dictators emerge.[14] Fascism may be closer to our portals than we think, as the recent Watergate experience should have taught us.

The mainline Protestant churches have been slow to recognize this peril. They tend to be vocal opponents of repressive "law-and-order" government, but they themselves have failed to understand the truth that if we are to resist a fascist drive for order, we must find ways of helping people gain control over their own lives. At a time when the Protestant churches should have been developing relatively firm positions on a variety of moral issues pertaining to everyday practical living, they have gone in the opposite direction. They have developed an alliance with various anticultural psychologies and psychotherapies, taken simplistic and unsophisticated stances with regard to openness and expressiveness. In trying to avoid what would appear as moralism, they have in general maintained a low profile on a wide range of practical moral issues, taking no position and offering no real guidance. In a pluralistic and rapidly changing society, there are strong pressures on all institutions—especially churches—to maintain a broad common denominator on practical issues. It is easy for the ethics of "do your own thing" to pervade even the province of organized religion.

CODA

Important questions relevant to the position taken in these chapters have gone unanswered.[15] Our goal here has been a limited one—to suggest that practical moral inquiry is an important dimension of care in a Christian context. By putting my emphasis on *moral inquiry* rather than on the rigid application of unexamined rules, I hope to avoid the charge of moralism. Yet by respecting the practical wisdom of the past and emphasizing the importance of culture and tradition, I hope to balance the accent on inquiry with the settling influence of the best in moral reflection from earlier times. By emphasizing the relevance of early Christianity—both what is distinctively Jewish and what is distinctively

Christian—I have pointed to a mode of existence that may have great importance for life in complex industrial societies. When the Jewish penchant for practical moral rationality is mixed with the emphasis on the in-breaking of the kingdom of God, a unique combination of life orientations are brought together. Jewish styles of practical moral thinking give us patterns, pathways, procedures, and systems of normative conduct. Christian expectations about the coming of the kingdom destructure these normative patterns, relativize them, free us from the oppressiveness of past guilt, open us up to new possibilities, and liberate us to develop an even more workable order for a newer age. Pastoral care must necessarily swing back and forth between these emphases, concentrating on one pole and then on the other. It must never abstract itself completely from the claims of either side, but must willingly specialize in one or the other as circumstances seem to dictate.

The goal of these chapters has been to sensitize us once again to the moral context of all care and especially the moral context of pastoral care. It has been my intention to swing the pendulum back in the direction of a moral concern, to argue for a rebirth of practical theology, and to plead for a heightened sensitivity to the implications for civilization of what we do in our care for one another.

Notes

CHAPTER I

The Contexts of Care

1. Talcott Parsons and Robert Bales, *Family, Socialization and Interaction Process* (Free Press, 1955), pp. 28–33.

2. Peter Berger speaks about the normative order of society under the rubric of "plausibility structures." Situations of rapid social change undermine these symbolic plausibility structures and put the normative symbolic order under strain, if not crisis. See his *The Sacred Canopy* (Doubleday & Company, Inc., 1967), pp. 17, 147–171, 154–155.

3. William Clebsch and Charles Jaekle, *Pastoral Care in Historical Perspective* (Prentice-Hall, Inc., 1964), pp. 30–31.

4. Seward Hiltner, to my knowledge, was the first to use the word "eductive" to refer to a mode of counseling that attempted to educe resources from within the troubled person. He closely associated it with a "client-centered" or Rogerian style of counseling. See his *Preface to Pastoral Theology* (Abingdon Press, 1958), pp. 151–154.

5. Karl Menninger, *Whatever Became of Sin?* (Hawthorn Books, Inc., 1973), pp. 223–230.

6. Robert Bellah, "Religious Evolution," *American Sociological Review*, Vol. 29, June 1964, pp. 368–369. Bellah seems to be suggesting that "world rejection" and the concern with individual salvation are responses to certain levels of social complexity and structural differentiation.

7. Max Weber, *The Protestant Ethic and the Spirit of Capitalism* (Charles Scribner's Sons, 1958), pp. 79–92.

8. *Ibid.,* pp. 98–110.

9. *Ibid.,* pp. 111–112, 229. That Weber hangs his entire Protestant ethic thesis on an assessment of the role of pastoral guidance in handling the problems of troubled people worrying about their election seldom has been noticed, especially by specialists of pastoral theology. Richard Baxter's *Christian Directory* appears to be a central source for this judgment. It should also be noticed that Weber took with him his concern for the role of religious counselors in his other studies on ancient Judaism, the religion of India, and the religion of China.

10. James Luther Adams, " 'The Protestant Ethic' with Fewer Tears," in *In the Name of Life: Essays in Honor of Erich Fromm,* ed. by Bernard Landis *et al.* (Holt, Rinehart & Winston, Inc., 1971), pp. 174–192.

11. Weber, *The Protestant Ethic,* pp. 128–154; also see *From Max Weber: Essays in Sociology,* tr. and ed. by Hans H. Gerth and C. Wright Mills (Oxford University Press, 1958), pp. 302–322.

12. Talcott Parsons, *Social Structure and Personality* (The Free Press, 1964), pp. 196, 278; for another analysis of how certain aspects of modern counseling and psychotherapy have conformed with the value assumptions of "middle-class" life and the Protestant ethic, see John Spiegel, "Some Cultural Aspects of Transference and Countertransference," in *Mental Health of the Poor,* ed. by Frank Riessman *et al.* (The Free Press, 1964), pp. 303–320. The belief that ascetic rationalism has continued to exert influence on American life in the twentieth century, at least during the early decades, does not also entail the idea that the Lutheran concept of calling and the Calvinist concept of predestination are consciously subscribed to by large portions of the population. In fact, it is Parsons' belief that the Protestant ethic to a great extent has been secularized and has lost its theological justifications, and that largely only its mode of relating to the world (instrumental activism) remains. It should be noted that I make no empirical claims for the dominance of the Protestant ethic in recent American history. For a summary of recent research on the status of the Protestant ethic in contemporary American society, see Gary D. Bouma, "Recent 'Protestant Ethic' Research," *Journal for the Scientific Study of Religion,* Vol. 12, July 1973, pp. 141–155. Bouma shows that most of this research is inconclusive, poorly conceived, does not really measure religious beliefs, and therefore can really say nothing about the relationship of religious beliefs to values in everyday life. For evidence that the Protestant ethic hypothesis is still

alive and kicking in social science literature, see S. N. Eisenstadt (ed.), *The Protestant Ethic and Modernization* (Basic Books, Inc., 1968).

13. Psychoanalysis has given rise to countercultural values not primarily in the work of Freud, which is on the whole somewhat conservative, but through what Philip Rieff calls the "remissive" interpreters of psychoanalysis such as Wilhelm Reich, Norman Brown, Herbert Marcuse, etc. Jung's emphasis on the balancing and compensatory power of the "archetypes" and Rogers' emphasis on the corrective influence of "organismic valuing" get closer to the anti–Protestant ethic values about which I am speaking.

14. Don Browning, *Atonement and Psychotherapy* (The Westminster Press, 1966). The theology of acceptance developed in this earlier book is not in contradiction to the spirit of the present book. I am here simply filling out the larger context of social, theological, and anthropological principles without which a theology of acceptance and forgiveness becomes meaningless.

15. Daniel Day Williams, *The Minister and the Care of Souls* (Harper & Brothers, 1961); Thomas Oden, *Kerygma and Counseling* (The Westminster Press, 1966), and *Contemporary Theology and Psychotherapy* (The Westminster Press, 1967); Gregory Baum, *Man Becoming* (Herder & Herder, Inc., 1970); and Paul Tillich, "The Impact of Pastoral Psychology on Theological Thought," *Pastoral Psychology,* Vol. 11, Feb. 1960, pp. 17–23.

16. Parsons, *Social Structure and Personality,* pp. 274–275.

17. *Ibid.,* p. 265.

18. *Ibid.,* pp. 270–271.

19. *Ibid.,* pp. 277–279.

20. *Ibid.,* pp. 283–291.

21. These are features thought by the Rogerian school to be characteristic of psychotherapeutic relationships. It is also claimed that these elements are common to all psychotherapy. See Carl Rogers, "A Theory of Therapy, Personality, and Interpersonal Relationships as Developed in the Client-centered Framework," in *Psychology: A Study of a Science,* ed. by Sigmund Koch, Vol. III, *Formulations of the Person and the Social Context* (McGraw-Hill Book Co., Inc., 1959), pp. 184–256.

22. Victor Turner, *The Ritual Process* (Aldine Publishing Company, 1969), pp. 94–97, 102–107.

23. *Ibid.,* p. 94.

24. *Ibid.*

25. *Ibid.,* pp. 94–95, 106.

26. *Ibid.,* p. 94.

27. *Ibid.,* p. 107. Turner writes: "What appears to have happened is that with the increasing specialization of society and culture, with progressive complexity in the social division of labor, what was in tribal society principally a set of transitional qualities 'betwixt and between' defined states of culture and society has become itself an institutionalized state. . . . Transition has here become a permanent condition." The implication of this remark is that in complex societies, partially because of this complexity, the dialectical relation between structure and liminality sometimes becomes broken. It is clear to me that Turner believes that this has happened in some of the "salvation religions" (Christianity, Buddhism, Hinduism, Islam), which have been the religions of higher, complex civilizations. One can even detect a value judgment in Turner to the effect that this is an unfortunate state of affairs, possibly limiting the social relevance of these religions.

28. Martin Buber, *I and Thou,* tr. by Ronald Gregor Smith (Charles Scribner's Sons, 1958).

29. Rudolf Bultmann, "The Historicity of Man and Faith," *Existence and Faith: Shorter Writings,* tr. by Schubert M. Ogden (Meridian Books, Inc., 1960), pp. 92–110.

30. Arthur Deikman, "Deautomatization and the Mystic Experience," in *Altered States of Consciousness,* ed. by Charles Tart (Doubleday & Company, Inc., 1972), pp. 25–46.

31. Turner, *The Ritual Process,* p. 129.

CHAPTER II

Roots of Care: In Judaism and Early Christianity

1. Parsons, *Social Structure and Personality,* pp. 277–283.

2. Max Weber, *The Sociology of Religion,* tr. by Ephraim Fischoff (Beacon Press, Inc., 1963), p. 28.

3. Marcel Mauss, "A Category of the Human Spirit," *The Psychoanalytic Review,* Vol. 55 (1968), pp. 461–462.

4. Weber, *The Sociology of Religion,* pp. 152–163.

5. *Ibid.,* p. 28; Gerth and Mills, *From Max Weber,* p. 272.

6. *Ibid.*

7. Parsons, *Social Structure and Personality,* pp. 295–300.

8. Gibson Winter, *The Suburban Captivity of the Churches* (The Macmillan Company, 1962).

9. Harvey Cox, *The Secular City* (The Macmillan Company, 1965).

10. John T. McNeill, *A History of the Cure of Souls* (Harper & Brothers, 1951) (hereafter cited as *HCS*); Clebsch and Jaekle, *Pastoral Care in Historical* Perspective (hereafter cited as *PCHP*); Henri Ellenberger, *The Discovery of the Unconscious* (Basic Books, Inc., 1970); Jerome Frank, *Persuasion and Healing* (Schocken Books, Inc., 1963); Ari Kiev (ed.), *Magic, Faith, and Healing* (The Free Press of Glencoe, Inc., 1964); Turner, *The Ritual Process;* Victor Turner, *The Drums of Affliction* (Oxford University Press, 1968); Claude Lévi-Strauss, *Structural Anthropology* (Doubleday & Company, Inc., Anchor Books, 1963).

11. Philip Rieff, *The Triumph of the Therapeutic* (Harper & Row, Publishers, Inc., 1966); Paul Halmos, *The Faith of the Counsellors* (Schocken Books, Inc., 1970); Kurt Back, *Beyond Words* (Russell Sage Foundation, 1972).

12. Weber, *The Protestant Ethic,* pp. 71, 119, 154, 193–194.

13. Weber, *The Sociology of Religion,* pp. li., 166, 169; Gerth and Mills, *From Max Weber,* pp. 325–326.

14. Weber, *The Sociology of Religion,* pp. xlix–1, 169–175; Gerth and Mills, *From Max Weber,* pp. 324–326.

16. Weber, *The Sociology of Religion,* p. lii; Max Weber, *Ancient Judaism,* tr. and ed. by Hans Gerth and Don Martindale (Free Press, 1952), pp. 254, 343. Weber saw Judaism as more world-affirming than Reformed Protestantism and less critical of the good things of this world. But it still had the intentional, active, and transformational attitudes toward this world which were, in part, marks of the inner-worldly ascetic.

17. Weber, *The Protestant Ethic,* pp. 98–99.

18. Weber, *The Sociology of Religion,* pp. l-li; Gerth and Mills, *From Max Weber,* p. 291.

19. Weber, *Ancient Judaism,* pp. 3, 13–23.

20. *Ibid.,* p. 3; Weber, *The Sociology of Religion,* p. liii.

21. McNeill, *HCS,* p. 11.

22. Weber, *Ancient Judaism,* pp. 169–178.

23. *Ibid.,* p. 178.

24. *Ibid.,* p. 179.

25. W. D. Davies, *Introduction to Pharisaism* (Fortress Press, 1967), p. 13.

26. *Ibid.,* p. 13; Weber, *Ancient Judaism,* pp. 388–389. In discussing

the rationalism of the Pharisees, Weber makes a distinction between speculation and practical-ethical rationalism. "However, the rejection of philosophical rationalism was correlated with a practical-ethical rationalism characteristic of petty bourgeois strata. Practical everyday needs and 'common sense' dominate the discussion and resolution of controversial issues."

27. Davies, *Introduction to Pharisaism,* p. 17.

28. Jacob Neusner, *Invitation to the Talmud* (Harper & Row, Publishers, Inc., 1973), p. xix.

29. McNeill, *HCS,* pp. 7, 11.

30. *Ibid.,* p. 11.

31. *Ibid.,* pp. 2, 6; Weber, *Ancient Judaism,* p. 269.

32. Weber, *The Sociology of Religion,* pp. 59, 69; *Ancient Judaism,* pp. 267–296.

33. Weber, *The Sociology of Religion,* p. 77.

34. Anthony Wallace, *Religion: An Anthropological View* (Random House, Inc., 1966), p. 181.

35. McNeill, *HCS,* p. 70.

36. Erwin Goodenough, *The Psychology of Religious Experiences* (Basic Books, Inc., 1965), p. 105.

37. *Ibid.,* p. 109.

38. *Ibid.,* p. 111.

39. McNeill, *HCS,* pp. 79–85.

40. John Cobb, *The Structure of Christian Existence* (The Westminster Press, 1967), pp. 116–117.

CHAPTER III

Roots of Care:
In Christian History

1. Clebsch and Jaekle, *PCHP,* pp. 8–9.

2. *Ibid.,* p. 12.

3. This is the general point of view of McNeill's *HCS.*

4. Clebsch and Jaekle, *PCHP,* p. 15.

5. W. D. Davies, *Paul and Rabbinic Judaism* (London: S.P.C.K., 1948), p. 323. The position of these lectures is in essential agreement with Davies' view of the role of the Torah in the early church. He writes of Paul: "But if our thesis is correct, this is exactly what we do find in Paul,

the application to the Person of Jesus of those concepts which Judaism had reserved for its greatest treasure, the Torah, so that we felt justified in describing the Pauline Christ as a new Torah."

6. II Thess. 3:6–14.

7. I Cor. 7:8–9.

8. I Cor. 7:39–40.

9. McNeill, *HCS,* p. 85.

10. Clebsch and Jaekle, *PCHP,* p. 17.

11. McNeill, *HCS,* pp. 90–91.

12. Clebsch and Jaekle, *PCHP,* p. 21.

13. McNeill, *HCS,* p. 105; Arthur Lovejoy, *The Great Chain of Being* (Harvard University Press, 1937).

14. Clebsch and Jaekle, *PCHP,* p. 21.

15. *Ibid.*

16. *Ibid.*

17. Weber, *The Religion of India,* tr. by Hans Gerth and Don Martindale (The Free Press of Glencoe, Inc., 1958), p. 6.

18. *Ibid.,* pp. 9–15.

19. Anselm, *Cur Deus Homo* (Edinburgh, 1909).

20. James Barclay, *Foundations of Counseling Strategies* (John Wiley & Sons, Inc., 1971), p. 123.

21. Benjamin Nelson, "Self-Images and Systems of Spiritual Direction in the History of European Civilization," in Samuel Klausner (ed.), *The Quest for Self-Control* (The Free Press, 1965), p. 70.

22. Clebsch and Jaekle, *PCHP,* p. 60.

23. Nelson, "Self-Images and Systems of Spiritual Direction," *loc. cit.,* p. 67.

24. *Ibid.,* pp. 70–71; Gustaf Wingren, *Luther on Vocation,* tr. by Carl Rasmussen (Muhlenberg Press, 1957).

25. Weber, *The Protestant Ethic,* p. 19.

26. *Ibid.,* pp. 99–128.

27. *Ibid.,* p. 111.

28. *Ibid.,* pp. 48–51.

29. Liston Mills, "The Relationship of Discipline to Pastoral Care in Frontier Churches, 1800–1850: A Preliminary Study," *Pastoral Psychology,* Vol. 16, Dec. 1965, pp. 22–34.

30. *Ibid.,* pp. 24–25.

31. McNeill, *HCS,* pp. 178, 184.

32. Hiltner, *Preface to Pastoral Theology,* pp. 48–49.

33. Clebsch and Jaekle, *PCHP,* pp. 30–31.

34. Most of the major theoreticians of contemporary pastoral care in the Protestant churches have been influenced to a great extent by Rogerian counseling, even though most of them are not confined by this one perspective. Even if they advocate styles other than the Rogerian, they seldom go beyond the eductive point of view. In this sense they partake of the Rogerian sensibility, if not always following Rogers' particular approach. See Seward Hiltner, *Pastoral Counseling* (Abingdon-Cokesbury Press, 1949); Wayne Oates, *Protestant Pastoral Counseling* (The Westminster Press, 1962); Carroll Wise, *Pastoral Counseling* (Harper & Brothers, 1951).

35. Adams, "The Protestant Ethic with Fewer Tears," *loc. cit.,* pp. 174–190.

36. *Ibid.,* p. 185.

37. Ernst Troeltsch, *The Social Teaching of the Christian Churches,* tr. by Olive Wyon (Harper & Brothers, Harper Torchbooks, 1960), Vol. II, p. 602.

38. David Little, *Religion, Order, and Law* (Harper & Row, Publishers, Inc., 1969).

39. Winthrop Hudson, "Puritanism and the Spirit of Capitalism," *Church History,* Vol. 18 (1949), p. 14. In this important article, Hudson also makes a critique of Weber's use of the writings of Richard Baxter as evidence that pastoral advice in Puritan circles supported intense worldly activity as a way of overcoming doubt about one's salvation. Hudson's article is helpful in placing Baxter in the context of his larger social teachings, which clearly subordinate personal economic profit to higher social responsibility. But on the other hand he quotes important passages in Baxter which suggest that between two paths of activity of equal dignity, it is a refusal "to be God's steward, and to accept his gifts" if one does not choose the more lucrative path. (Hudson, *loc. cit.,* p. 11.) This may be an admission on the part of Hudson large enough to sustain Weber's position.

CHAPTER IV

Culture, Religion, and Care

1. Paul Tillich, *The Protestant Era* (The University of Chicago Press, 1948), p. 57; Clifford Geertz, *The Interpretation of Cultures* (Basic

Books, Inc., 1973), pp. 87–125; Benjamin Nelson, "Self-Images and Systems of Spiritual Direction," *loc. cit.,* pp. 52–55.

2. Philip Rieff, *Freud: The Mind of the Moralist* (Doubleday & Company, Inc., 1959); and David Bakan, *Sigmund Freud and the Jewish Mystical Tradition* (Schocken Books, Inc., 1965).

3. Benjamin Nelson, "Systems of Spiritual Direction," *Criterion,* Vol. 11, Spring 1972, p. 17.

4. Howard Clinebell, *Basic Types of Pastoral Counseling* (Abingdon Press, 1966), p. 31. Clinebell conveys this by saying in one place that "creative teaching methods" are "indispensable to much pastoral counseling."

5. *Ibid.,* pp. 31, 90–91.

6. *Ibid.,* p. 45.

7. Thomas Oden, *The Intensive Group Experience* (The Westminster Press, 1972).

8. Back, *Beyond Words,* p. 77.

9. *Ibid.,* pp. 31–46.

10. George Simpson, *The Meaning of Evolution* (Yale University Press, 1949), pp. 224–228; for a discussion of how population theory of evolution might be applied to the field of personality theory and developmental psychology, see Robert LeVine, *Culture, Behavior, and Personality* (Aldine Publishing Company, 1973).

11. This distinction roughly corresponds to Heinz Hartmann's distinction between autoplastic and alloplastic adaptation. Heinz Hartmann, *Ego Psychology and the Problem of Adaptation,* tr. by David Rapaport (International Universities Press, Inc., 1958), pp. 26–27.

12. Talcott Parsons' introduction to Weber's *The Sociology of Religion,* p. li.

13. Talcott Parsons, Reneé C. Fox, and Victor Lidz, "The Gift of Life," *Social Research,* Vol. 39, Autumn 1972, p. 369.

14. *Ibid.*

15. Clifford Geertz, "The Impact of the Concept of Culture on the Concept of Man," in *The Interpretation of Cultures,* p. 49.

16. *Ibid.*

17. Theodosius Dobzhansky, *The Biology of Ultimate Concern* (The New American Library of World Literature, Inc., 1967), pp. 109–134.

18. *Ibid.* This is also the general position of Pierre Teilhard de Chardin, *The Phenomenon of Man,* tr. by Bernard Wall (Harper & Brothers, 1959), pp. 243–244.

19. See especially Alfred North Whitehead, *The Function of Reason* (Beacon Press, Inc., 1958), p. 8.

20. In addition to Dobzhansky's *The Biology of Ultimate Concern,* see L. Charles Birch, *Nature and God* (The Westminster Press, 1966), and L. Charles Birch, "A Biological Basis for Human Purpose," *Zygon,* Vol. 8, Sept.-Dec., 1973, pp. 244–258.

21. David Bakan, *The Duality of Human Existence* (Rand McNally & Company, 1966).

22. Alfred North Whitehead, *Process and Reality* (Harper & Brothers, Harper Torchbooks, 1960), pp. 255–279.

23. Arthur Deikman, "Bimodal Consciousness," *Archives of General Psychiatry,* Vol. 25, Dec. 1971, pp. 481–489. I want to thank my student Jack Engler for pointing out this article and suggesting to me the concept of "destructuring" as a handy way of speaking about how dominant modes of consciousness are relativized in certain types of religious experience as well as therapy.

24. Robert Ornstein, *The Psychology of Consciousness* (The Viking Press, 1972), p. 52.

25. *Ibid.,* pp. 107, 108–118.

26. Paul Ricoeur, *Freedom and Nature,* tr. by Erazim Kohák (Northwestern University Press, 1966), p. 13. Throughout his writing, Ricoeur uses his concept of diagnostic to indicate the possible relationship between a scientific fact of biology or psychology to levels of human meaning. The relationship he says is not one of equivalence, but is a "diagnostic" relationship. This means that the objective level and the level of subjective meaning might be symptomatic of each other—e.g., symbols of wholeness, unity, and presentness being symptomatic of right hemisphere functioning or, in turn, right hemisphere functioning showing up in the appearance of symbols.

27. By evolutionary theory of religion, I do not mean to suggest affinity with those theories which see a simple progression from early to later expressions of religion such that the early is lower and the later is higher or more complex. Nor do I associate myself with positivistic points of view which say that religion is associated mainly with primitive mentality and will disappear as mankind evolves into maturity. I mean only to suggest that religion as the serious or ultimate dimension of culture gives solidarity to man's orientations to adaptation.

28. For a recent statement of this point of view see, Eugene G. d'Aguili and Charles Laughlin, "Biopsychological Determinants of Reli-

gious Ritual Behavior," *Zygon,* March 1975.

29. *Ibid.*

30. Wallace, *Religion: An Anthropological View,* pp. 220–224.

31. For an excellent case study of the work of a shaman in a primitive society see Victor Turner, "A Ndembu Doctor in Practice," in Kiev. (ed.), *Magic, Faith, and Healing,* pp. 230–264.

CHAPTER V

Toward a Model of Care

1. James Gustafson, *The Church as Moral Decision Maker* (Pilgrim Press, 1970).

2. Arthur Danto, *Mysticism and Morality* (Basic Books, Inc., 1972), p. 114. For Danto, Confucianism comes the closest of any of the Eastern religious philosophies to a truly moral and ethical perspective on life.

3. It should be noted that throughout this section I will use interchangeably the words "moral" and "ethical." Both words refer to the possibility of relatively free individual and corporate moral action which can have some actual consequences in narrowing the gap humans perceive between the actual and the ideal. In the next chapter I will move to a somewhat more specialized understanding of the meaning of the words "moral" and "ethical."

4. "Identity confusion," which is a type of confusion of values, as a factor in emotional distress, has been a constant theme of the writings of Erik Erikson. See my *Generative Man* (The Westminster Press, 1973), pp. 166–178.

5. Parsons, *Social Structure and Personality,* pp. 258–291.

6. Wallace, *Religion: An Anthropological View,* p. 175.

7. *Ibid.,* p. 223.

8. Those readers who are aware of the position I developed in *Atonement and Psychotherapy* may be interested to know how the position developed in the present book—with the strong emphasis on the Jewish context of Christianity, moral and ethical inquiry, and the general emphasis that the Judeo-Christian tradition is an ethical type of religion —squares with this earlier work. In brief, the answer is that here I am developing a two-factor or dialectical theory of the sacred. The sense of the sacred moves back and forth between structure and liminality or communitas. In *Atonement and Psychotherapy* I was developing the

aspects of Christianity associated with liminality and communitas, i.e., acceptance, forgiveness, and love, and their possible correlation with dimensions of the psychotherapeutic relationship as described by Rogers —unconditioned positive regard, empathy, and congruence. I do not think it is necessarily a repudiation of this former concern to place it now in a broader and, I believe, more accurate context.

9. Parsons, *Social Structure and Personality,* p. 331.

10. McNeill, *HCS,* p. viii.

CHAPTER VI

Method in Religious Learning

1. Sigmund Freud, "Obsessive Acts and Religious Practices," in Sigmund Freud, Collected Papers, Vol. 9, *Character and Culture,* ed. by Philip Rieff (Collier Books, 1963), pp. 17–26.

2. Morton Lieberman *et al., Encounter Groups: First Facts* (Basic Books, Inc., 1973).

3. Back, *Beyond Words,* p. 34.

4. Kenneth I. Howard and David Orlinsky, "Psychotherapeutic Processes," *Annual Review of Psychology,* Vol. 23 (1972), p. 630.

5. See John W. White (ed.), *What Is Meditation?* (Doubleday & Company, Inc., Anchor Books, 1974), and Tart (ed.), *Altered States of Consciousness.*

6. Ornstein, *The Psychology of Consciousness,* pp. 49–74.

7. Weber, *Ancient Judaism,* pp. 69–74.

8. Davies, *Introduction to Pharisaism.*

9. Neusner, *Invitation to the Talmud,* p. 224.

10. *Ibid.*

11. *Ibid.*

12. In my book *Generative Man,* I investigated at some length the understanding of the developmental regularities of human life put forward by Erik Erikson. Erikson claims that there are certain developmental stages strongly tied to biological maturational schedules. But Erikson would agree with the position set forth here that these stages of development are not rigidly determined, that they require favorable environments to activate, and that there are always elements of individual decision relevant to each stage of emergence. For Erikson, it is important to know the schedules of development, but one never simply relies, for

purposes of adaptation, on the instinctual and developmental tendencies of the body. But a fuller explication of the relationship between the anthropology of "generative man" and the position set forth in the present book must await another time.

13. Menninger, *Whatever Became of Sin?,* pp. 223–230.

14. Erich Fromm, *Escape from Freedom* (Farrar & Rinehart, Inc., 1941).

15. Since these chapters are directed primarily to a popular audience, I have not entered into technical discussion more than was necessary. But the more specialized reader may appreciate some hint about my position on several issues implied but not discussed here. First, I consider the ethical position reflected in these pages as representing a kind of "rule-utilitarian" approach to ethics. This means that I believe that the consequences of an act are an important, although not the exclusive, perspective from which its moral quality should be judged. Yet this position is rule-utilitarianism (with emphasis on the *rule*), because I emphasize the importance of developing traditions of rules that seem to have an "average expectable" applicability to a certain range of situations and cases. Of course in a rapidly changing society, situations change and so must the rules that govern them. But rule-utilitarianism still puts great emphasis on both the likely applicability of old rules to current cases as well as the importance of developing new rules and new traditions when old ones finally prove unworkable. The emphasis on rules, their maintenance and development, distinguishes my position from all varieties of situation ethics, which has been the main partner of modern pastoral care theory insofar as the latter has had any alliance whatsoever with formal ethical theory.

Second, the more specialized reader may be interested in knowing that the distinction I have maintained between "health" and "morality" in these chapters can be relaxed somewhat if the issues are viewed from the perspective of a small minority of contemporary psychologies. Especially is this true from the perspective of Erik Erikson's contribution, which is, I believe, more properly thought of as a "moral psychology"—a psychology that describes the nature and development of the moral individual. Erikson's concept of "generativity," which I have discussed at length in my book *Generative Man,* bridges the gap between health and morality. Generativity is a virtue that goes beyond health in that it is primarily aimed at enriching and strengthening the cycle of the generations. But generativity is also built on a host of other developmental modalities such as trust, autonomy, and initiative, which, although they are not distinctively moral virtues, are indispensable developmental precursors to the more distinctively ethical stage of generativity. In the more technical jargon of formal ethical theory, Erikson has given us a kind of "trait-utilitarianism," which would correspond to the rule-utilitarianism that I briefly discussed above.

Third, the more specialized reader may be interested in some preliminary discussion of a suggested method in the development of a practical theology, which I have called for several times in these pages. Those interested are referred to my recent article entitled "A Prolegomenon to a Practical Theology of Aging," in *Pastoral Psychology,* Dec. 1975.

253
B885

LINCOLN CHRISTIAN COLLEGE AND SEMINARY

83466

3 4711 00231 3825